Karrie knows that freedom is not [ ] d *Fully Alive*, she gives us the tools needed to win. From reclaiming what darkness stole from our childhood to practical steps for healing, this book is more than just words on a page. It's a war cry for the life we've always longed for.

TONI J. COLLIER, SPEAKER; PODCAST HOST;
AUTHOR, *BRAVE ENOUGH TO BE BROKEN*

My girl Karrie has written a transformative and deeply healing book. If your story is filled with pain and hopelessness that you can't seem to shake, do yourself a favor and read this masterpiece. This book deeply spoke to and challenged me in ways I didn't even know I needed.

KAIT TOMLIN, BESTSELLING AUTHOR; DATING
COACH; FOUNDER, *HEART OF DATING*

Karrie Garcia is one of my favorite teachers. *Free and Fully Alive* is more than a book—it is the how-to of true transformation, hope, and peace that Karrie passes on to us from her own experience. Read it and learn how to live.

LISA WHITTLE, AUTHOR, *GOD KNOWS*;
PODCAST HOST; BIBLE TEACHER

Karrie is one of the most funky, honest, life-giving people you can cross paths with. In dark seasons, you need a friend you can laugh and cry with—Karrie is that friend! I'm thankful to Karrie for so vulnerably sharing her story and for giving us a road map back to who we are meant to be.

ADAM WEBER, LEAD PASTOR, EMBRACE
CHURCH; AUTHOR, *LOVE HAS A NAME*; HOST,
THE CONVERSATION WITH ADAM WEBER

I sometimes wonder "Am I really free?" as I consider the concept of false freedom in my own journey of recovery from alcoholism. Karrie helps unpack this concept and demonstrates what it looks and feels like to journey to freedom. Readers will gain the awareness that freedom is a journey, not a destination, as Karrie brilliantly encourages us to do the work to get free. If you want to know what freedom looks like—if you want to know what freedom feels like—then you want to engage on this journey with Karrie Garcia to live truly free and fully alive.

IRENE ROLLINS, AUTHOR, *REFRAME YOUR SHAME*;
PASTOR; SPEAKER; RECOVERY ACTIVIST; MARRIAGE
EDUCATOR, TWO=ONE MARRIAGE MINISTRY

In *Free and Fully Alive*, Karrie Garcia points us to the transformative truth that our past doesn't disqualify us from the love of God. Karrie creates a sacred space for honesty that points us to hope and healing. With tenacious transparency and solid biblical teaching, Karrie invites us to fully embrace every part of our story and reclaim it all for God's glory.

CASSANDRA SPEER, BESTSELLING AUTHOR; BIBLE
TEACHER; VICE PRESIDENT, HER TRUE WORTH

Karrie Garcia is on a mission to see everyone experience healing and freedom through the power of story work! *Free and Fully Alive* is a blueprint for releasing past traumas, breaking cyclical patterns, and stepping fully into the life God has for us.

CHERYL NEMBHARD, AUTHOR, *BRAVE: THIS IS US*;
SPEAKER; DIRECTOR, WOMEN SPEAKERS COLLECTIVE

Karrie is truly a gift to the kingdom of God. I have benefited tremendously from Karrie's ministry over the years. Her profound ability to intensely hold space and "lean in" to minister deeply to people's souls is unparalleled. This book does such a great job of communicating her tender heart for all of us to experience true restoration, wholeness, and victory. Do yourself a favor, kick up your feet and start reading.

CHRIS BROWN, PASTOR, THE WELL; AUTHOR, *RESTORED:
TRANSFORMING THE STING OF YOUR PAST INTO PURPOSE FOR
TODAY*; HOST, *LIFE. MONEY. HOPE. WITH CHRIS BROWN*

Karrie artfully takes us on a pilgrimage to unearth our stories and break cycles of false freedom so we can experience deep healing, leading us to courageously step toward who we're genuinely created to be. This book strips the darkness of its power, breaking bondages in a way that will not only set us free but also cause us to live fully alive.

ANDI ANDREW, AUTHOR; BIBLE TEACHER; PODCAST HOST

Karrie has written a book that invites us to consider our pain and suffering as well as a God who is radically committed to our healing. She brings together her passion for story work, her love of Scripture, and her devotion to a God who has offered a path to freedom. This book was a delight to encounter.

CATHY LOERZEL, COFOUNDER, THE ALLENDER CENTER; STORY WORK COACH AND SPEAKER; COAUTHOR, *REDEEMING HEARTACHE*

Karrie has delivered a must-read for discovering your purpose through the uniqueness of your life's story. Her honest approach and knowledge of God's Word will shine hope on your pain and bring fullness to your life.

JEN JONES, SPEAKER; AUTHOR; COACH

KARRIE GARCIA

FREE

&

FULLY
ALIVE

RECLAIMING THE STORY OF WHO
YOU WERE CREATED TO BE

ZONDERVAN
BOOKS

ZONDERVAN BOOKS

Free and Fully Alive
Copyright © 2023 by Karrie Garcia

Requests for information should be addressed to:
Zondervan, *3900 Sparks Dr. SE, Grand Rapids, Michigan 49546*

Zondervan titles may be purchased in bulk for educational, business, fundraising, or sales promotional use. For information, please email SpecialMarkets@Zondervan.com.

ISBN 978-0-310-36644-7 (softcover)
ISBN 978-0-310-36646-1 (audio)
ISBN 978-0-310-36645-4 (ebook)

Cover design: Mario Garcia / Faceout Studio
Cover illustration: Max9545 / Shutterstock
Interior illustrations on pages 85, 91, 93, 98: Karrie Garcia
All other interior illustrations: Brandon Steele
Interior design: Denise Froehlich

Printed in the United States of America

23 24 25 26 27 LBC 5 4 3 2 1

To my husband, Mario.

It was you who lovingly walked with me through countless sleepless nights, held my tears when I had no words, and never stopped believing that healing was for me. My soul has found peace because of your persistent pursuit of my wandering heart, and through that I met a piece of Jesus that had felt far away until his love, through you, showed me a new way.

CONTENTS

PART 5: CONNECTION WITH GOD

PART 6: CONNECTION WITH OTHERS

PART 7: A CALL TO HOME, A CALL TO YOU

ACKNOWLEDGMENTS

First I would like to thank my three children, Ryder, Rocco, and Roma, for being the catalyst for my healing. You keep me honest and have been the driving force behind my belief that my healed heart will provide an avenue for your own healing. You three are God's redemptive gifts that gave me the courage to face my past and believe for something better. I love you.

Additionally, my deepest gratitude to Dr. Dan Allender and Cathy Loerzel for creating the Allender Center. It was there that the depths of my story were held in such a way that for the first time I felt like my life made sense and hope was attainable. What the two of you have created has changed the trajectory of my life and in turn has changed the lives of those I have the privilege of caring for. This book, in part, is the outcome of the work you are doing to change people's stories of harm to hope. My words will never match my gratitude.

An additional thanks goes to Melanie Turnipseed for the late nights and countless calls to help me navigate this book and help me birth its words. Also special thanks to my agent, Rachel Jacobson from Alive Literary Agency, for plucking me out of obscurity and believing that my voice deserves to be heard. I could not end these acknowledgments without thanking my amazing editor, Carly Kellerman, who partnered with me to bring this book to life. Her care and desire for the reader to receive the hope and transformation I wanted to convey allowed this book to become what it is today. Lives will be changed because of her valiant *yes* to this work.

I am deeply humbled by all those who have stood beside me and helped me reclaim who I was created to be.

PART 1

FREE
& FULLY
ALIVE

CHAPTER 1

SETTING THE STAGE

I was five years old when I made my stage debut. It was a kindergarten class presentation of *Hansel and Gretel*, and my role was so insignificant that I don't remember it. But I do remember that it seemed, to this young drama queen in the making, I was headlining on Broadway. I was the star, and it was my time to shine. The curtains rose, some magic happened, and in the blink of an eye, the performance was over. My *moment* was over. The reason I was put on earth was over. Devastated and desperate to soak up every ounce of attention I could, I felt my body fill with adrenaline and my heart scream, "It can't be over!" I broke from our class lineup backstage, dodged my teacher's attempt to stop me, and rushed back toward the stage. "The show will go on!" I thought. It took me a few minutes to find the curtain opening (why is that so hard to do?), but the second I did, I broke through the heavy velvet with my arms dramatically extended as I belted my made-up song: "I'm a ham! I'm a ham! My mom says I'm a ham!"

Dooo Doo Do . . . I can still hear that tune in my head to

this day. It was my songwriting debut. I strutted across that stage and sang with everything in me, bending, bowing, and poking my dimples because I saw Shirley Temple do that once—and she knew her stuff! I got through maybe three lines of this master-piece before Mrs. Hansen, my teacher, came onstage with a look of horror on her face. She dragged me offstage while I waved and blew kisses to my adoring fans. As I waved, everyone cheered. (Or at least they did in my mind. I'd later find out that no one cheered; most were just confused and shocked.) My parents sat in the front row, stunned but not altogether surprised. I fondly remember thinking, "Look how great the world is and how great it is that I'm in it! My parents must be so proud." Do I remember if my parents were proud? No. Do I remember if I got in trouble? No. All I know is, looking back, I'm proud of that little girl.

My days as that precocious little girl seem like a lifetime ago. *Man*, that girl had some moxie! She was a performer, an entertainer, a make-others-better-er. She was filled with won-der and amazement. She had dreams and desires and believed in all the goodness she held. She was fearless and innocent at the same time. She knew what she was called to do and took the bull by the horns. She was mighty and silly and fun and saw the world uniquely. When she rebelled, it was often because being tied down was to be caged, and she knew there was more for her out there. I admire five-year-old me. In many ways, she was my best self. Unfortunately, it didn't take long for the best things about that little girl to get lost in a sea of attacks. Why? Because the essence of that little girl—a little girl who was free and fully alive—is who God created me to be, but there is an Enemy utterly determined to keep me from the glory I possess.

I grew up thinking I had lost that little girl. For so much of my life I felt I was being told to sit down, be small, stop speaking up—your voice doesn't matter. Dimming my God-given qualities—the tenacity, the passion, the leadership, the sense of wonder and fun—distanced me from my purpose and left me feeling isolated, stuck, and unable to fulfill God's call on my life as a speaker and a guide toward freedom. But I'm discovering that the fierce performer, the one filled with wonder, adventure, and childlike play, still exists within me. And the young passionate dreamer still exists within you too. That's what this book is about—finding freedom and abundant life through the courageous act of reclaiming the story of who you were created to be.

I was taught that God wants us to live freely, but I never understood what that kind of freedom meant or felt like. It seemed like a good idea in theory, but elusive—I had no idea *how* to grab a hold of it. Granted, there were seasons of my life when I *felt* free but really wasn't. If freedom meant being carefree and uninhibited, that kind of freedom was mine during the years I was addicted to drugs (more on that later). I was free to make the decisions I wanted and do whatever made me feel good in the moment, but that freedom never brought me peace. I was free but not fully alive. I was enslaved to my own freedom—which was really counterfeit freedom.

So what does biblical freedom mean? The freedom God offers throughout Scripture is freedom from the enslaving power of sin in our lives. The Enemy uses sin to obstruct our relationship with God, keeping us from experiencing abundant life in God. Biblical freedom allows us to reclaim what the Enemy has robbed from us so we can live the story of who God created us to be.

By contrast, worldly freedom is the ability to do what we

want, when we want. When Adam and Eve were in Eden, they were free to choose whether to eat from the Tree of Knowledge of Good and Evil. But choosing to eat from it brought consequences—death.

Paul gives us a clear idea of this whole freedom thing and defines what biblical freedom truly means and doesn't mean. He wrote in 1 Corinthians 6:12, "'I have the right to do anything,' you say—but not everything is beneficial. 'I have the right to do anything'—but I will not be mastered by anything."

What does this mean for you? This means Jesus set you free so you can stand firm in his power to live a life that is free *and* fully alive, not so you can be bound to the things of this earth. He wants you awakened to a life that can hold both hurt and hope. A life that cries out in grief but can whisper gratitude in the same breath. This kind of freedom allows you to have faith in Christ but still experience human fears. You can bring them both before the cross, where his grace, love, and mercy can cover you and empower you.

There's a not-so-fun part of finding freedom, though. If you want to be truly free, you must first recognize the places where you have settled for counterfeit freedom. You must awaken to the reality that parts of your story have been hijacked by an Enemy who wants you to believe that freedom lies in your power to choose, rather than through the transformation of your heart. Once you recognize where this Enemy has attacked your story, you can begin the work of reclaiming those places so you can experience the life abundant and return to who you were created to be.

We all come with stories—some good, some bad, and some really hard. Our deepest desire is to be known and loved, but our stories often include times when we were not known for who we really are and definitely were not fully loved. And yet we can't escape the belief that maybe, just maybe, there's hope for our stories, that maybe our lives can be redeemed and we can emerge as the free little ones we once were. Our spirits hold a curiosity around hope. Even if that hope has sunk within us, it's still there, calling to us, speaking of what was and what could be. This longing comes from the desire to create and dream and play. It's as if our spirits know life wasn't supposed to be this way—we weren't made for pain and despair. We were designed for something greater. Our spirits long for Eden.

Our spirits long for the goodness and intimacy they were created to experience. They long for the wonder of the unknown and the mystery of what could be. Our spirits seem to know something our brains don't—that we were made for abundant life—but our brains won't let us engage because of fear of disappointment or failure or rejection. It's our spirits that keep leading us to the reckless hope of trying again. All it takes to keep going is a willingness to be honest, to invite God into the story, and to allow some trustworthy people to witness your story in a way that enables your heart to be seen and held. Something dynamic and supernatural begins to happen. Life starts to have color. The puzzle pieces of your broken story come together. You are awakened to a God who sees you in the hard and the holy, and you realize you are loved. God meets the great longing of your soul within the recesses of the stories you bear—which he wants to redeem.

I have studied the Bible and the brain for years—research was my way of making sense of the trauma in my life—and I've discovered that these areas of study complement each other. My spirit tells a story, and my body tells a story—and my work has caused the two stories to align and hope to blossom. My studies took me to the Allender Center, led by Dr. Dan Allender. I had read many of his books and knew I needed to learn directly from him. I had no idea what I was getting into. I went mostly to enhance my understanding of Scripture and the brain so I could bring more concrete tools to all of you. This motive was well intended, but the Lord had other ideas. The premise of the center's work is to find places of harm in your story and to understand more clearly why you do what you do. All this work is done using the framework of God's Word. I was in! I had zero clue what it meant to "dive" into my story—I had zero idea I even had a story—but God drew me to the center knowing that I would find the freedom I longed for and in turn help others who desired freedom too.

Before the first four-day weekend, I was required to submit a story from my childhood. It was to be no more than six hundred words and as detailed as possible. "Think of a story that always stands out to you, one that has weightiness to it." That was the extent of the directions we were given. Plus we were told we'd share the stories with each other in small groups—which I do all the time, so no biggie. So I gave it a go—but the process was more than I bargained for.

As I sat in my group, preparing to listen to others and eventually share my own story, a wave of fear rushed over me. I felt disconnected from my body. I wanted to run, and thoughts flooded my mind: "Who are these people? How can I trust them? What will they think of me?" On the outside, I kept it as cool as possible, but I was freaking out on the inside. I mean, I came here to learn tools to help others, not to dive deeper into my own story. Plus, I had already done years of inner work, so it all seemed stupid. But feeling that way was my way of covering up my fear.

For four straight days I listened to six women share their stories. We held space for each other, we cried, and we offered questions to help each other gain more insight. The Allender Center has a saying: "You can't take anyone further than you're willing to go yourself." I knew that for me to be a voice of hope for others, I needed to allow myself to have a voice, one that showed vulnerability in the hardest parts of my story—not so much the big traumatic moments but the small ones that had a powerful impact on how I saw myself and the world around me. It was going to be brutal.

When it was my turn to share, I gripped the chair and could barely breathe. My survival brain said, "Run! These people are not to be trusted. Sharing this is weakness, and you are *not* weak." I was caught in a battle between my mind and my body. For the first two days, I couldn't remember the names of the people in my group and could barely remember their stories. It was as if my brain had gone offline in preparation for sharing my story. Did you know this is something your brain does in traumatic situations? It's a remarkable feature to protect itself. The prefrontal cortex (one of the parts of your brain that stores memory) pretty much shuts down, time slows, and memory gaps occur, all to preserve a sense of sanity during trauma. Well, this was happening to me. I was in a fog. People were offering insights that illuminated parts of my story and naming how it had affected my life. I knew we all had experienced harm and traumatic moments, but I had no idea my stories were keeping me from being the me God created me to be. This exercise opened my eyes to the Enemy's work on my behavior, thoughts, and feelings; my anxiousness and depression and need to over-achieve began to make sense. As brutal as those first few days were, I felt seen. God was exposing the darkness, and yet he was right there with me. For years I had been preaching and teaching on acknowledging feelings, naming needs, and inviting God into our lives as a means of experiencing freedom. But through the honesty of this story work, I connected to what was going on *inside me*, allowing God to speak truth into the stories that were keeping me bound and slowly letting myself connect with others to experience the fullness of my healing. By sharing my stories, a path forward emerged and I took courageous steps toward truly loving who I was created to be.

I've since done several years of training with the Allender Center, and it's always hard connecting to myself, God, and others, but the freedom that comes is worth the work. One night after a particularly challenging training day, I was lying in my hotel room and prayed, "God, this is so hard. If you aren't in this or if I've made a mistake, let me know." Engaging in all aspects of my story was causing a lot of disruption in my life, and I needed to be sure that the work I was doing at the Allender Center was indeed where God wanted me. I fell asleep and woke up around three o'clock in the morning with a vision of a large statue being pulled down with ropes and crumbling to the ground. A voice spoke to my heart, and I heard it as clear as day: "I will have no other gods before me." The voice was not mean but matter-of-fact. I knew at that moment that the work of revealing the truth in my stories was breaking idols and bondage in many areas of my life. I felt as if I was coming home—home to me, home to the God who created me, home to truth and to a purpose fueled by hope.

This book will speak to the deepest part of you, the part that knows there is more. It will reawaken you to the little one who held such promise and who knew that, if given the chance, they could offer such goodness to the world. The journey we'll be taking together isn't just a journey to be free—God wants more than that for you. It is a journey to living free *and* fully alive. When Jesus spoke of an abundant life, he meant a life that overflows. A life so full it will pour out and over others. A life in which you and the Father partner together to bring the goodness of the Lord to the land of the living (Psalm 27:13). In this life you will not only reconnect to your giftings but also discover your calling. Engaging in this work will bring you back to who you were created to be, but it will also awaken a holy defiance on behalf of others in the particular areas in which you have been assaulted. You will want to expose the lies of the Enemy in the same places you have been lied to. This work changes generations, heals communities, and awakens hope. The work is hard, but the outcome is an unquenchable fire that desires to partner in the rescuing of hearts.

CHAPTER 2

RECLAIMING CHILDLIKE WONDER

The concept of childlike wonder likely isn't new to you, especially if you've grown up Christian. There are sermons and songs dedicated to this concept. Matthew 18:1–3 tells us, "At that time the disciples came to Jesus and asked, 'Who, then, is the greatest in the kingdom of heaven?' He called a little child to him, and placed the child among them. And he said: 'Truly I tell you, unless you change and become like little children, you will never enter the kingdom of heaven.'" In this passage, Jesus is telling us to be completely dependent on him, to rely on him the way children rely on their parents. He tells us that this childlike dependence is the key to entering the kingdom of heaven, where we will experience abundant life with him. But what does it *really mean*? Why does God want us to remember what it was like to be children when we are adults who have striven to grow up?

God is calling you back to the young dreamer within you,

asking you to remember when you last felt that childlike trust in him and his purposes, because he's the same loving Father to you today as he was then. God created you for a purpose, but walking in that purpose requires igniting the passions he's planted in you, the passions you pursued with abandon as a child.

Specifically, he's calling you to depend on him the way a child depends on their parents: with faith, imagination, dreams, wonder, and awe. *Awe*. When was the last time you looked at God in awe the way a five-year-old looks at a brightly lit Christmas tree or brand-new bicycle? Allowing ourselves to return to our younger selves not only reminds us of our unique characteristics but also allows us to be in awe of God as we delight in who he created us to be.

In our own human ways, we make a mess of our lives—or for many of us, the mess was done to us. The work of embracing freedom and living fully alive will mean understanding that although you have been harmed and you have all but forgotten that courageous little one, they are still in there and God is not done yet!

Some of the most courageous freedom-giving work happens when you remember who God created you to be, by going back into the stories where your life's harmful narratives first began. As I shared before, the little Karrie who danced on the stage was far from my memory for years. But as I dove into this work and my story, I began to love that little girl. Over time, I realized that the memory of her—and many other memories of when I was free and fully alive—had been clouded by memories that the Enemy had latched on to, times when he whispered lies to keep me from who I was created to be. The boldness within me, the glory I radiated, and the innocence I carried were a threat to his kingdom, and he was determined to shut me down. He whispered lies such as "Good girls don't shine too brightly," "Stay in line and be like the rest," and "Your bigness makes people uncomfortable, so be a little less you."

What's crazy is that my first memory of these attacks was that very day when I stepped onto that stage. What was a free and fully alive moment was instantly clouded by what I thought was disapproval from my parents and my teacher. Their reactions became whispers that told me, "Be less you!" and "You are an embarrassment!" Over the years, I have felt this way with my parents, teachers, friends, and coworkers. And every moment I felt a twinge to be less like myself, the Enemy collected it as data to use against me. He'd say, "See, every time you are *you*, people leave. They pull their love away, so stop it." When you hear these kinds of whispers long enough, they become a contract you unknowingly sign. A contract you begin to live up to. With this agreement in place, you are now bound to those beliefs, and the lies feel like truth. You begin to filter your whole life through this grid of lies, and you wonder where God is and why you are not free. It's maddening!

We all have stories of harm. Whether you lived in a good home or a terrible home, the Enemy did not pass you by. You experienced harm and assault the moment you showed the free and fully alive self you were created to be. The process of undoing this harm can feel scary, maybe even unnecessary. You may have thoughts like "What's done is done; why go back?" or "If I open this up, I'll never recover." This is exactly what Evil wants. He wants to make you believe this is the best it will be. He wants you to forget the glory you bear and settle for a life watching from the sidelines—to believe the whispers that started so early on, and to allow the lies you have been told to sink deep and fester. He wants to take you out.

We all have our own origin stories; these are the narratives that shape how we think about ourselves, God, and the world. I grew up in an evangelical home. My father was a pastor, and my mother was the quintessential pastor's wife. She was beautiful and sweet and never missed a Sunday. She sat in the front row and wrote copious notes in her Bible. Some Sundays, when she was feeling a tad wild, she would volunteer on the worship team and play her egg shaker! This was a big deal for our conservative roots. I know this version of my mom well. She was consistent, well dressed, always smiling, and standing by my dad's side as the congregation exited the church. This version, the one everyone saw, was true in the sense that I believe she truly wanted this to be her true self. The real truth, though, is that my mom was the loneliest person I knew. She was a shell, beautiful on the outside but hollowed by pain. I watched for years as she deprived her body of care. It seemed the only time she felt worthy was when people complimented her on how skinny she was or how beautiful or young she looked. Her mouth told the story that people wanted to hear—that she was fine, we were fine, and God was good—but her body told another story. Beyond the frailness and unhealth left by her pervasive eating disorder, her body was ravaged by the decades of shame and pain she held alone.

I watched shame destroy my mom. I remember thinking, "Why can't you get better? Just stop doing what you're doing, and everything will be okay!" In my adolescent mind, I thought if she stopped her eating disorder behaviors, all would be right with the world. The reality is that those behaviors brought my mom relief, but they didn't bring her healing. Like many of us, my mom was stuck in what I call a "cycle of false freedom"—a repeating pattern of lies and behaviors that keeps us from experiencing the true freedom God provides (more on this in the next chapter). She had Jesus—and she had behavior modifications to help her "get through" her pain and shame. But she didn't have a strong enough connection with herself to understand the root of her needs. Without understanding what she needed, how could she bring those needs to God? Instead, she believed all she needed was validation that she was beautiful and assurance that her performance was successfully masking her pain and shame.

The places of your story that keep you captive must be examined and brought into the light—this is the only way to strip darkness of its power. Every other attempt will leave you feeling like a failure, which is the goal of the Enemy—to make you spin your wheels and stay on a cycle of false freedom, finding behaviors that satisfy for the moment but keep you from the path to true transformation. The work of true healing requires bringing tenderness to our stories, to our bodies, and to our souls. We must be honest about our stories—the experiences and moments that have shaped who we are—and allow ourselves to connect to what is really going on within us.

Here's the deal—I'm not asking you to do anything I haven't already done. I've been searching for the abundant life for as long as I can remember. I have tried every way to figure out the key, and I have landed here, in the simple, not-so-simple engagement of my story. It's within the terrain of my life's stories that my glory and my downfall lie. It's within these stories that I was both harmed and protected. Our stories tell the truth, and when the truth is exposed it sets us free. Your story has been waiting for you to take the courageous step to turn and face the places you've wanted to avoid, to awaken to the stories you've wanted to minimize, and to offer care to the stories that need to be felt.

You, my dear reader, are a survivor. You have encountered much that should have taken you out, but you are still standing, with breath in your lungs and maybe even a flicker of hope in your heart. Perhaps you have already done some of the work of engaging your story, but I encourage you with this: God is not done. There is more healing and more glory for you to behold. Your sanctification to become more like Christ is not an arrival; it's a journey. So even if you think you have already done this work, there is so much more. Ask God to fill you with his vision for freedom. Want *all* the freedom God may have for you. Settle for nothing less than to be surprised by God. Surrender your fear and control and story to Jesus and watch as he begins to reclaim what the Enemy has stolen. It's in this honest work that heaven will invade earth and you'll get glimpses of eternity within your heart.

Throughout this book, I will provide moments for you to pause, reflect, and pray. These moments are not intended to be rushed but to be savored. Use them to offer care as your body needs it. To invite Jesus into the fragile, sacred places of your heart. This is a journey you and I are going on together, one that will be led by the Holy Spirit. So there may be times you need to pause and pray. I have offered a few prayer prompts, but you can always say whatever is on your heart.

As you journey, I pray that the peace of God will cover you and that hope will rise from the depths of your story. It is here that you'll see the glory of God and the riches he has for you. As you begin this journey, I offer you a promise from Philippians 1:6: "Being confident of this, that he who began a good work in you will carry it on to completion until the day of Christ Jesus." Jesus won't leave you unfinished. His promise is to continue his work within you and bring it to completion. The best news I can offer is that freedom is for you and an abundant life awaits, right here on earth. This doesn't mean the absence of difficulties, but it surely means an all-knowing, all-encompassing God will be your comforter and your guide. The journey awaits, and you have been called for such a time as this.

> *Dear Lord, I'm ready. I will choose to trust you with this process, even though I may be experiencing fear or hesitation. I will listen to the voice that leads me to hope and not to fear. I will allow my heart to be seen, even the places I've kept covered. You created me and breathed life into my lungs, and it is because of this truth that I will offer my life to you. I want a life that is awakened to all you have for me. I want to see more of you. I don't want to stay stuck anymore, and I don't want to be bound to the lies I've believed for so long. Help me, Holy Spirit, to discern your voice and your guidance. Use this book to guide me to see more of you and the truth you have for me within your Scriptures and within your presence. Thank you for your pursuit of me—even when I run, you somehow still find me. Here I am, Lord, tired of running. Have your way. In Jesus's name, amen.*

PART 2

COURAGEOUS & FREE

CHAPTER 3

THE CYCLE OF FALSE FREEDOM

Can I share a random fact about me? I *love* a bacon gouda sandwich from Starbucks. Truthfully, I'm eating one right now as I write this. I have eaten this sandwich pretty much every morning for two years straight. When I walk into my local Starbucks, they usually have my black tea and sandwich ready for me. I have even preached a sermon using an illustration about this sandwich! And now I'm laughing as I write this, because I'm about to do it again.

I went through a tremendously difficult season recently. During that time, I would wake up thinking, "If I can just get to Starbucks and have my sandwich and tea, I will get through the day." Truthfully, it worked. The thought of this sandwich and my tea and the routine and structure they brought soothed me and helped me keep going. This was around the time I was doing some deep story work, which was bringing up pain from my past. I was overwhelmed by the pain of losing my mom, my dad's remarriage, and a flood of memories that were causing deep wounds and stories of harm from my past to resurface. My world was turned upside down, and I wanted something, *anything*, to numb my feelings and bring temporary comfort. This routine and this sandwich were my tools to keep me going and distract me from what I was feeling every morning when I got up. I would start with a breakfast sandwich and move to other food items throughout the day to keep me far from what I was feeling.

This cycle began slowly but soon became what I craved in order to not feel the pain I was dealing with. Over time, this simple routine became bondage. I was unhealthy and unhappy, and although I wanted to heal these pains, I had no idea how. So I opted for a cycle and routine that numbed me so I didn't have to fully engage the stories I was facing.

Using food as a distraction is something I was taught from a young age. I grew up in a home where food was used as a coping mechanism and a means to not have to feel what was happening. My mom had a pervasive eating disorder that controlled every aspect of her life. Her bulimia started when she was thirteen, and by the time she had me, she was so steeped in this addiction that much of what we could and couldn't do revolved around her ability to have places to binge and purge. Even as a young girl I knew something was wrong, but I didn't know the extent until I was thirteen. That's when I first heard the word *bulimia*. Day after day, month after month, year after year, my mom lived in a cycle of shame and hatred for herself. When the shame and hatred were too much, she would numb her pain by binging, and she would try to control her weight and her emotions through purging.

Here's the truth: as humans, we don't do anything that doesn't have some sort of payoff. There must be a reward for our behavior, even if just a temporary one, or we wouldn't do it. Our brains and our bodies want to avoid pain, especially if there is no safe place to process it. My mother lived a life of verbal abuse and neglect as a child. You would never have known it by looking from the outside, but the stories she told and the ones I experienced showed me the shadow side of what it meant to be a little girl in her home. Her eating disorder was applauded by the world—or rather, not so much the disorder itself but what it brought: a skinny body and youthful appearance. It also gave her a sense of love and acceptance. The problem was the world loved and valued her because of her beauty, and the beauty was linked to her addiction. She gained not just the applause of men but also the adoration of her mother and the delight of her father. None of these people actually loved my mom for who she was; they loved her for what she brought to them. But my mom experienced a payoff for all the harm she was causing herself. Even though the payoff—that feeling of acceptance—lasted only a moment, she believed that was all there was. Shame will drive us to do harmful things to our bodies and minds if those actions will provide a temporary reprieve from pain and momentary acceptance from others. My mother wasted away for years so she could experience a few moments of relief before shame came flooding back in with full force. Her addictive behaviors allured her with the promise of release, only to leave her bound to a cycle that was slowly killing her.

It might be easy for you to read this and think, "Wow, that's a hard story." Maybe you even feel relief that you don't have it "that bad." It's easy to look at someone with a blatant addiction and not identify with them because that's not you. We relegate addiction to substance abuse and eating disorders, but truthfully, addiction can happen anytime you routinely use something to numb your pain instead of going to God to heal it. Remember my sandwich story? I was repeating the same cycle as my mom. The sandwich itself wasn't my addiction, but it fed a cycle of food being the place I turned to for soothing and comfort so I didn't have to deal with my heart. The sandwich had no moral value, but it soon became the start of my everyday cycle of eating to numb my feelings. I looked forward to it. I would think about it the night before. I mean, friend, *it's a sandwich!* But isn't that the way it works? My mom started wanting to lose a little weight when she was twelve, and that desire consumed her so much that by the age of fifty she weighed one hundred pounds and frequently considered taking her life. No one thinks this will be the case for them, but this is the way of an Enemy who wants to entice you by offering something that brings only temporary relief, so you have to come back to it again and again until you are so bound you can't see a way out.

My story is filled with this type of cycle—and as mentioned in the previous chapter, I call it the "cycle of false freedom." The cycle of false freedom is a cycle of lies and behaviors that keep us from fully receiving God's love and *true* freedom. These lies and behaviors may make us *feel* better as we attempt to move forward, but as is true with all cycles constructed by man or schemed by the Enemy, we achieve zero growth and often end up even worse than we started. The lie is that this cycle will change our hearts and relieve our pain, but true heart transformation does not happen this way. Our behavior might change, but deep inside our hearts we still feel lost, broken, and ashamed.

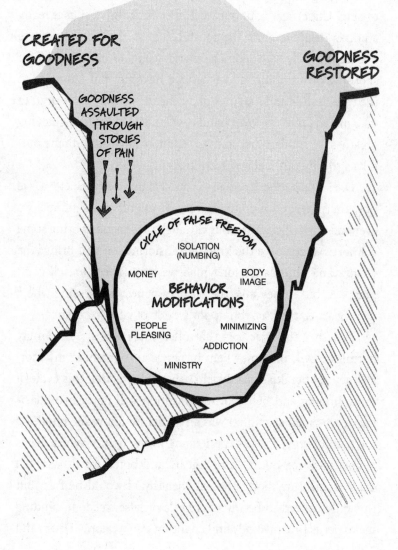

James wrote about how the Enemy draws us into this cycle of false freedom. James 1:14–15 (ESV) says, "But each person is tempted when he is lured and enticed by his own desire. Then desire when it has conceived gives birth to sin, and sin when it is fully grown brings forth death." What desire is James referring to here? Underneath our outward, specific sinful desires is really an inner desire to avoid the painful feelings of a life where we're not feeling fully satisfied. The world seems to offer immediate soothing or numbing, and when we have not put language to the true desires and longings of our heart, we may be enticed to take matters into our own hands, whether that means achieving greatness or human successes to feel more alive or numbing ourselves so we don't feel anything at all.

Does this sound familiar to you? We put forth the effort, we pray the prayers, we go to church, we attend small groups, we even memorize Scripture, but although these actions bring some comfort, we don't see the kind of transformation that brings the victory and abundance for which we long. These are all good practices, but if they take the place of honestly assessing where your heart is, they set you up for a cycle of false freedom.

Whether the practices that offer you relief are seemingly harmless, evil, or somewhere in between (remember my morally neutral breakfast sandwich?), the reality is that this cycle of self-numbing and behavior modification will never bring lasting peace or satisfaction. I was an addict for ten years, numbing the pain of what I was experiencing in my home. When drugs almost took me out, I shifted gears and opted for fitness. If I could control my body and eat "healthy," I would be free. But this only proved to be my next cycle of false freedom, binding me to perfecting my body and counting every calorie. Drugs and fitness may seem like totally opposite responses to my pain, and one might look like the obviously better choice, but both practices stemmed from the exact same pain and posture of my heart. By trying to circumvent the hard work of facing my trauma and my story, I filled my life with distractions aimed at happiness. Spoiler alert: it doesn't work that way.

One of the hardest cycles I have had to break was that of ministry. This cycle was hardest because from the outside it looks so spiritual and holy. This cycle told me that if I served enough, read enough, and offered all of myself with no regard to caring for the body, mind, and spirit God gave me, then I would achieve the fully alive life the Bible talks about. Make no mistake, the Enemy was working cleverly here. He enticed me with the applause of others, a carrot dangling in front of me for more followers, and a platform to elevate myself, all in the name of serving God. The lie told me, "This will make the pain go away! You will find the abundant life you have been searching for here."

You see, it doesn't matter if your aim is to "kill it for the kingdom" or chase the next high—when your true goal is to avoid pain, you will ultimately find yourself alone, depleted, and caught in a cycle that was supposed to offer freedom but is actually a snare of the Enemy. The behaviors in the cycle become the idol to which you are bound. As we see in James, the danger of continuing the cycle is that it will lead you not to life, but to death. It may not be physical death you encounter, but a spiritual and emotional death, where life is gray and the fully alive experience you longed for feels like a pipe dream.

To live free *and* fully alive, we must understand where these cycles play out in our own personal lives. Some may be more obvious than others, but everyone engages in cycles of false freedom to avoid feeling and healing what is in the depths of our stories. These cycles promise us freedom but leave us exhausted, striving, and desperate. We get into an endless spiral as we *attempt* to be victorious on our own—and it's important that we recognize this spiral in our own lives so we can break free of it.

How might cycles of false freedom show up in your life? We all have vices, whether they are at church, work, or home—or whether we're chasing drugs, achievements, or social media followers. You name it, and the cycle is the same. Here's an example of how it might manifest in a weekly cycle:

- **Sunday**—Church! Worship! Closeness with God! Community! You feel full, happy, and ready to take on the week.
- **Monday**—Lists, lists, lists. With the energy from Sunday, you write your to-do list, goal list, and lists of other lists you need. God feels near, but you also feel the urge to perform, to "kill it," and to do all the right things—in the name of Jesus, of course.
- **Tuesday**—Euphoria begins to wane. Goals feel overwhelming. The Enemy begins to whisper hateful things: "Who do you think you are? You're never going to get all of that done. You were stupid for thinking you could."
- **Wednesday**—The shame spiral begins. You feel like a fraud, believing you'll never be anything more than a slacker, bad parent, unloving spouse, and unrealistic list maker. So you fake it. You believe if anyone knew the real you, they wouldn't want to be around you, so you cover *you* up.

- **Thursday**—These emotions are too much to bear. You numb the feelings of disappointment and shame with whatever vice you have—maybe it's alcohol, drugs, cleaning, binge-watching TV, scrolling through social media, or gossiping with a friend.
- **Friday**—Self-justification begins to set in. The guilt of not doing all the things you set out to accomplish begins to fade, and you tell yourself, "It's fine. I didn't need to do any of that stuff anyway. My value is not in the things I do; it's in being happy!"
- **Saturday**—What you're feeling isn't real happiness; it's escapism. Jesus feels far, fatigue is overwhelming, and your internal dialogue feels like chaos. You may cycle through the feelings of the last six days all in this one day. It feels impossible to break free from your vice. You feel shame, fear, indifference, or maybe even rage.
- **Sunday**—Church! Worship! God! Community! You view church as your much-needed shot of adrenaline to power up for the next week.

This example is in the form of a weekly cycle, but these cycles can play out over any period of time. A cycle can rear its head whenever external, temporal things give us a false sense of hope and value. It may happen over a week or over a year, but either way it keeps us further from who we were created to be and from the Creator who made us. If we live this kind of addictive lifestyle, the results will always be the same—counterfeit hope and counterfeit value.

I am so thankful God chose to tell us in detail the story of the Israelites. Their story paints a picture of the continual pull to enter back into the cycle of false freedom. In Exodus 32, we see that after Moses had been on Mount Sinai with God for quite some time, the people became fearful and restless. They said to Aaron, "Come, make us gods who will go before us. As for this fellow Moses who brought us up out of Egypt, we don't know what has happened to him." Even though God had been faithful by delivering them from Egypt, they felt the need to take matters into their own hands because their longings and desires were skewed by fear. They lacked courage because they failed to remember the power of God in their story. They wanted freedom, but freedom meant they had to surrender and trust when it seemed easier to fall back into familiar pagan rituals. We experience the same struggle today that the Israelites experienced thousands of years ago. We want to control our lives rather than fully surrender to a God we don't truly know or trust— feels pretty darn close to what the Israelites experienced. They were scared, traumatized humans who had little faith yet were loved by God. Sound familiar? God is leading us to the promised land where our dreams, hopes, desires, and abundant life await. Living in shame, counterfeit hope, and performative faith is not the life God has for you.

For dreams to take root in our lives, we must end the nasty cycle that's tearing us up inside. A powerful first step toward healing is to get honest with yourself and, in that honesty, to offer kindness to your wounded places, places where stories of harm have kept you stuck and caused you to operate the only way you knew how. We are too comfortable with condemnation. Beating ourselves up comes so naturally, doesn't it? Consider how often downright nasty thoughts about yourself pass through your brain. These thoughts perpetuate the cycle and keep you coming back to your vices to get a sense of relief so the nasty thoughts can go away. This breaks my heart for you. I have seen too many men and women succumb to this cycle of never-ending longing while never being fulfilled.

At this point, you may be asking, "What's really at stake? Why open my wounds only to feel the pain I've tried so hard to avoid?" These are fair questions. Many of us can't even imagine what being fully alive could feel like. We have been barely surviving for so long that it seems like that's all there is. Our capacity to dream and imagine has been clouded by a cycle that keeps us stuck and in need of temporary relief. But I didn't write this book just to give you some ideas that I hope you will implement to better your life—this is about life and death for us. James didn't write about this cycle just for you to think about these things in your spare time; he wrote about it as a warning. If you live out this cycle long enough, it *will* bring death.

I told you about my sweet, broken mom, the woman who thought being skinny and young and desired by people would bring her freedom. She was bound to a cycle that promised life but brought death, and it eventually led her to take her own life.

I lost my mom to a lie that she had believed for so long that it was where she put all her faith. This lie, this cycle, this avoidance of pain allowed the Enemy to say whatever he wanted until he convinced her that it would be better if she were no longer here. No one thinks in their early years that they will one day take their life or that they will live a life that is gray and hopeless. This happens when a person spends years bound to a cycle that keeps them far from the God who created them and loves them and wants to tend to the places of their heart that are fragile and wounded. I am motivated, dear reader, not to let one more person who crosses my path succumb to a cycle that will eventually end in some type of death, whether physical, emotional, mental, or spiritual. I have seen this type of hopelessness, and I have experienced it personally as well, but I have also seen what happens when we come to God honestly, step out of the cycle of false freedom, and offer our broken, fragile hearts before the Lord.

God wants to break this cycle for you. He does not lie, and when he says he has an abundant life for you, he means it. Perhaps you have believed for far too long that this life God speaks of is one you must *try* to attain. Your futile efforts have left you exhausted and beaten down, which has caused you to settle for "good enough." The best news that has ever been written is that God does not need your behavior to change for him to transform your heart. Let me say that again. God does not need your behavior to change for him to transform your heart. What he does need is your heart. *All of it.* The good, the hard, the ugly, and the honest. Giving him your heart means giving up control over your life and acknowledging that only God has the power to transform you. The first step in breaking the cycle of false freedom is admitting you are stuck in it in the first place. It's in this confession that you can be honest with God as to *why* you are where you are. It's here, in this honesty, that a ray of hope can shine through and darkness can begin to dissipate.

Once we're honest about our pain and shame, we can invite God into our story to restore and heal.

If you're ready to invite Jesus into your fragile places, say this prayer:

Dear Lord, thank you for loving me through every part of my story. Thank you for inviting me out of condemnation and into healing so that I may live free and fully alive. I invite you into every area of my heart, even the hidden places I've been ashamed to reveal. Please join me in my journey to living an abundant life. Amen.

CHAPTER 4

EMBRACE YOUR STORY

For years, I minimized my story. The pains of my life were too much to bear, so I numbed them by using drugs and climbing the popularity ladder to feel some sense of belonging and worth. Drugs and alcohol worked for a while . . . until they didn't. I was either going to die from my addiction or get help to stop it, and I chose the latter.

Once I got clean, I decided it was time to share my story with others (after a whopping four months of sobriety). I would be a good testimony for the Lord! There was a purity to this instinct—after all, God did help me and I did stop using drugs—but here's the problem: I never dealt with why I did drugs in the first place.

What motivates a thirteen-year-old girl to take her first drink behind a bush at an eighth-grade dance? Rebellion? A need to be liked? Just wanting to be wild? There was probably a little truth in all of those, but the overriding reality was my home was barren and filled with anger. Looking back, even before the drugs, I never had words to describe the pain I felt. I just knew I didn't like who I was very much, and I had better figure out a way to change. So I did—all the time. New interests, hobbies, hairstyles, boyfriends, you name it—I was trying to reinvent myself to find myself. Nothing lasted long before I was on to the next better thing. Even religions were possibilities for finding happiness. It was miserable. *I* was miserable. I was angry, volatile, unhappy, unfulfilled, and lonely. My actions were cries for help, and no one listened. "Fix your behaviors, fix your problems." This was the message I heard loud and clear, although within the walls of my home this mantra wasn't actually fixing anyone. If anything, our efforts to fix ourselves by changing our behaviors—whether through ministry or eating disorders or performance—only seemed to leave everyone in more and more isolation and pain.

Once I stopped using, I moved straight into a new addiction: ministry. My instinct was to downplay the bad parts of my story—to find God's goodness in everything and walk away scot-free from my hurt and pain, with a mission in mind. I was going to help others get off drugs and find Jesus! As you can imagine, it didn't work out that way. We are integrated beings. Our brains hold memory, and our early memories shape how we see life, love, and ourselves. My life was consumed by addictive behaviors that drove me to fit in any way I could and to escape the reality of the pain in my heart. If it wasn't drugs, it would be the allure of the stage I would stand on for Jesus. This would be the "thing" that would set me free. The irony of my taking a stage to perform for affection is not lost on me. But while my childhood self had used her gifts onstage out of a sense of freedom, my adult desire to return to the stage and use my God-given gifts was motivated not by freedom but by the need to perform to prove my worth to others and God. I moved from one addiction to another, from one behavior change to another; they all seemed to promise a way to living fully alive.

For many years, I was experiencing all this pain behind a pulpit. I was a youth pastor, and although I believed the words I was speaking, I had no idea how to live them out myself. I found myself desperate and rage filled. I was stuck but had no idea how to break free; I didn't even know if there was a way to break free. All the behaviors I had used to grab on to freedom failed, and nothing I tried brought any kind of lasting relief. I wanted out of whatever this life was. I did things I never imagined I would do, and I hurt people because I was hurt. I lived up to the beliefs I had about myself—I believed I was a fraud, that I was "too much," and through my actions I seemed to be trying to prove those beliefs true. In this state of mind, I hit my breaking point and started behaving in ways that eventually cost me everything—my ministry, marriage, close family relationships, everything gone. Everyone I knew saw me either as a sinner or as too much to deal with. I was alone, which for me was the worst place to be. I hated me. I had never wanted to end my life before this point, but I had run out of distractions to keep me from my feelings and from my hurt. I felt lost; I didn't know what to do. I cried out to God from the depths of my heart, but for many months, he seemed silent. I wrote and read and hoped for something to make the ache of my life go away.

I remember the moment when it all felt like too much. I was sitting in my studio apartment all alone, and the weight of my brokenness and shame was choking me out. I wanted to die. I wanted the overwhelming pain to leave, and in my anger, I wanted everyone to miss me. I rationalized (although there is no rationality in such situations) that maybe if I were gone everyone would finally see me and realize how I had been hurt-ing. Remember the story of me as a girl onstage, singing with zero fear? That little girl's desire to be seen and loved was still there inside me, but everything good and innocent was gone. Her glory had been stripped away, and I was left feeling a sense of utter hopelessness, death knocking on my door. It was in this moment I decided I was going to end it all. It's interesting how generational sin passes from generation to generation and how we are tempted to succumb to the same fate as our parents and grandparents. My plan was to take my life, in my car. I was sob-bing and just wanted the pain of my "disqualified" life to end. It was then that Jesus placed these words in my head and on my heart: "I see you, I am with you, take courage." I wish I could say I had giant-sized faith in that moment, but I didn't. I guess I had what Scripture refers to as mustard-seed-sized faith, and it moved the mountain of pain in my heart enough for me to seek the help I needed. I had to choose whether to hear the invitation and respond or to let my pain do its bidding. I chose to give God one more try, but this time I wasn't going to just get my behav-iors right—I was going to allow him access to my heart.

My pain shaped me to operate in ways that helped me toler-ate a broken world. I didn't start thriving in my life until I was able to acknowledge my pain, invite God into it, and then under-stand how God could use the pain of my story to awaken within me a call to guide others toward freedom and an abundant life.

Embracing your story takes work. I had to recognize that the story I was believing—that I was too much and needed to play small—was a lie. Then I needed to face my actual reality—that I was created to speak truth in boldness, in confidence, and with zeal. I had to shine an honest light on the hard parts of my life and acknowledge that they were what had prepared me to enter that reality. On the journey to be fully alive, you can't bypass your pain, because the painful places are where your purpose and calling began to form. When we bypass these crucial parts of our stories, we bypass the emotions we carry and the truth that God wants to meet us in all of it—in other words, we bypass the motivation behind our calling.

You want to walk toward true freedom? You must get honest. Easy enough, right? Actually, it's brutal. Honesty means choosing to uncover things we may or may not have known were there and face the ugliness of it all. My story, your story, and humanity's story are all riddled with pain and heartache. To many of us it seems easier to avoid those stories and leave them in the past where they happened. However, we now know that leaving these stories untended to means they get to continue to dictate our lives—they skew how we love and listen and lead. Staying away from the stories that have shaped us will hinder our healing. This is why the belief that we can just come to Jesus without inviting him into any of our past experiences, telling ourselves that all is good and forgotten, is bad theology—it doesn't work. Without honesty, we will not see our need for Jesus. Honesty exposes reality, allows for intimacy, and draws us closer to our needs and desires. And, as Jesus tells us in John 8:32, the truth sets us free.

You may have reservations about this whole honesty thing. You may be telling yourself one of two things: "If I open up, I will never recover," or the even trickier lie, "I don't really have a story; my hurt is minimal in comparison with others'." Both are lies from the Enemy to keep you from the truth of *your* story. Maybe your story is not as horrific as someone else's, but that doesn't diminish the pain you feel or your need for Jesus to offer care to the broken places in your heart so you can stop living a less-than-fully-alive life. Telling yourself that your story is not that big of a deal or avoiding it altogether is to continue to live a life controlled by your pain and brokenness. Essentially, the very thing you're wanting to avoid becomes the framework through which you live and love. *You are living out* your story of heartache if Jesus has not had access to your pain. There is a way out, a formula to follow, but you will need to stop dead in your tracks and turn and look at the places you have avoided or minimized. It's in those places that Jesus promises to meet you, tend to you, and heal you. The very places you have wanted to avoid because of what might happen if you face them are the very places that will set you free if you place them in the hands of God. The opportunity for freedom has existed within your story your whole life; the story has just been in the wrong hands. Your story in the hands of the Enemy will cause destruction, but your story in the hands of God will create freedom.

No matter how immense the pain you carry, you are loved by a good God who promises to meet you in your painful places. It's here that a fully alive life can take root and the possibilities of hope begin to rise.

> *Dear Lord, I invite you into the fragile places of my heart to be near me as I begin this journey of embracing and engaging my story. Please speak through the words on these pages and hold my heart as we go through this healing work together. In Jesus's name, amen.*

CHAPTER 5

A COURAGEOUS ACT

Asking God to show you your story takes courage. It's a brave decision to return to pivotal moments in your life to see how God was revealing who he created you to be—and it can be scary to realize that certain aspects of your created self have been stolen from you. We'll address this more in later chapters, so it's important that we first spend some time understanding what biblical courage looks like and how it will help you live life abundantly.

When Scripture speaks of courage, I think we often understand it as the absence of fear or harm; we think that, somehow, if we have enough faith, courage will come and we can avoid the fear of pain, but that's not true. We can't will ourselves to be courageous. To have courage is to intentionally step into the fear of the unknown and trust that what God says is true. Having courage is the first step toward living free and fully alive.

Let's be clear: courage is anything but being fearless. Being fearless is impossible. I mean, there are ways that I can fear less, but a total absence of fear is impossible to achieve. Courage means having strength in the face of difficulties such as pain or grief. Courage is walking *through* the pain, facing the grief, and withstanding the fear. We muster courage when we choose to trust God even in the unknown or in painful situations. In Deuteronomy 31:6, we're instructed to "Be strong and courageous. Do not be afraid or terrified because of them, for the LORD your God goes with you; he will never leave you nor forsake you." As Christians, we love to quote this verse. You might have it written on a bathroom mirror or a Post-it in your car. But let's be honest, how many times have you shouted this verse at yourself when even the tiniest bit of fear crept in—and it didn't work? Here's the thing about Scripture, friend: it's a full narrative of God's love, grace, and mercy, not just a book of quotes to get us through tough times. We must understand the context and characters to fully understand what God is revealing to us. So, let's look at the context of why Moses spoke the words in Deuteronomy in the first place.

Moses is one hundred and twenty years old, and his time is coming to an end. God has asked Moses to establish Joshua as the new leader of the Israelites, so Moses is giving a few final words to the people to encourage them for when Joshua eventually steps in. This transition should be easy enough, but we must remember the Israelites are a scared bunch and change has never gone well for them.

Let's pause here to fully immerse ourselves in this story. Imagine wandering in a desert for decades, constantly questioning God's goodness, following one man as your only hope. Then, imagine that this man is about to die and a new guy is going to step in. This is scary. It's easy for us to read the story in its context and see the amazing presence and goodness of God. But the Israelites only saw Moses and didn't know the end of the story. Moses was the man who had protected and led them and in whom they put their trust. Knowing he was about to die must have been terrifying.

Okay, back to Deuteronomy. So, Moses summons all the Israelites and begins to share about the transfer of power and leadership from him to Joshua. As we can now understand, this probably does not land well. The Israelites know Moses has been forbidden to go into the promised land, but now the reality is weighing on their minds and hearts. Moses has seen them through years of heartache and turmoil, so their grief must be at an all-time high. Not to mention they still haven't entered the promised land, and it looks no safer now than it did when they scouted it out many years ago. Moses sees their fear, he feels their fear, and because his life's purpose is to get these people to their rightful place, he is going to lay out the plan in the face of that fear. This is probably why Moses says, "Be strong and courageous." He's letting the Israelites know that although they'll have to fight, they won't be conquered; although they must trust a new leader, they won't be forgotten; and although they don't know what lies ahead, they can trust the Lord.

Having the courage to step into our stories is painful, I know. It musters up many emotions, especially fear. Our pasts have been hard and filled with trauma, and that can cause us to believe that stepping further into the story God has for us will only lead to heartache. How many times have we said to ourselves, "What's in the past is in the past. I can't go back and change it; I just have to move forward"? We believe these words are true because moving forward seems simpler, maybe even more hope filled. We numb out and go through the motions, hoping we will wake up one day feeling the sense of freedom for which we're longing. The truth is that God has been with you during every difficult season, waiting for an invitation to hold you in your grief. You may not have seen him at the time, but returning to those moments can awaken your spirit to the presence of God in every aspect of your story. Time and time again, the Israelites forgot who they were and *whose* they were. They forgot the promise God had for them; they forgot the moments of deliverance. Their forgetfulness led them to lack the courage to face what God was leading them into. Let's not be like the Israelites!

Every invitation requires a response; to step into freedom you must respond to God's invitation by saying, "Yes, you are welcome here." This "yes" invites God into the process of your healing. God wants an invitation into all the parts of you—the real, honest parts of you. He wants to be invited into where you are today, into what you feel, think, and believe, even if those beliefs feel scary or shameful. How can he transform your heart when the truest places of your heart are off-limits to him? Can God force his way in? Absolutely, but that has never been his approach. Just as it's our choice whether to have a relationship with him, it's our choice whether to invite him into our most fragile places.

Just as Moses charged the Israelites to have courage as they pursued their God-given destiny, God is saying the same to you. I meet many people who have big dreams and are filled with desire yet are utterly stuck in pain, shame, and condemnation from their past. They have forgotten the person God created them to be. Perhaps you know this feeling well. I'm so happy to tell you that God has an abundant life for you today. You need only the courage to say yes to the journey ahead.

Are you ready to say yes to beginning the journey to being free and fully alive? Say this prayer with me:

> *Dear heavenly Father, thank you for creating me to have childlike wonder. Thank you that you want me to live an abundant life, experiencing freedom and pieces of heaven on earth. God, today I invite you to help me remember the moments in my life when I was unabashedly who you created me to be. Please give me courage as I seek to love and embrace all of me. I invite you into the fragile parts of my story. Thank you for loving me in all of these moments. I love you. Amen.*

CHAPTER 6

AN ABUNDANT LIFE

U p to this point we've been getting honest about our stories, breaking our cycles of false freedom, and inviting God into our journey to become who he created us to be. Jesus clearly states in John 10:10 what the Enemy does to our lives, but he also tells us what God offers: "The thief comes only to steal and kill and destroy. I came that they may have life and *have it abundantly*" (ESV, emphasis added).

Jesus wants us to have life that is *full*—so we will now explore what it means to be *fully alive,* to attain abundant life here on earth. I'm talking about the "I can move mountains with the faith of a mustard seed" (Matthew 17:20), "I shine" (Matthew 5:16), "I'm living abundantly" (John 10:10) kind of stuff. Abundant life is a glorious idea, but often it doesn't feel attainable or sustainable. When was the last time you felt fully alive—like you were living abundantly?

For much of my early adult life, the abundant life that I heard about in church felt out of reach; it was as if abundant life was only meant for "the good ones." When I was younger, I believed with my whole heart that life was to be lived without fear and that I could do anything if I had faith as small as a mustard seed. My wide-eyed younger self sang, "This little light of mine, I'm gonna let it shine, let it shine, let it shine, let it shine!" At that time, I was all for this charge. "I will shine like the stars!" I thought. But somewhere along my storyline, the moxie and imagination of that idealistic little girl slowly faded. It's often the seemingly small moments that cause the most harm—like the time I was in a play in sixth grade, and I forgot the words and froze. As everyone laughed, I felt a piece of myself die; I never wanted to be seen like that again. A familiar whisper rang in my ear: "You will never measure up to your competitors. Why even try?" But the worst part wasn't my freezing on the stage; it was that there was no one there to comfort me in my pain. I was on my own. "I better toughen up, or things like this will keep happening to me," I thought. Moments like this made me so angry inside and so hurt that I wanted to numb the pain.

The whispers inside my mind multiplied until I was convinced I was disqualified to offer any good or to even let myself imagine the abundant life I had heard about in Scripture. The instruction to "let my light shine" felt hollow, meaningless, and unattainable. To shine, I would have to be someone I didn't believe I was anymore. But there was still fight in the girl. How would I find the freedom I longed for? How would I dispel the thoughts of hatred that whirled around in my head? How would I do right so I could feel right?

Achievement became my on-ramp to a cycle of false freedom that promised a whole and healed life. I just had to work hard for God and use the gifts he had given me to make his kingdom known. So, I started to *do*, to achieve, and to play the part of being good without ever really knowing what it meant to *be* good. I made my dad proud with every sermon I gave. People applauded my ability to speak with passion as I shared my redemption story of going from drug addict to Christ follower. "I was made for this; *this* must be the way to the fully alive life I'm searching for," I thought. This cycle of achievement worked—for a while. Then, like all the other behaviors I had tried, it left me once again alone and angry. God felt far away, and I felt exhausted trying to please everyone and be a "successful" Christian.

This is not an uncommon story. Teachings about the abundant life echo in church halls all around the world. These teachings often follow a riveting message that tells us, "There is an Enemy who prowls, waiting to devour us. But don't worry, God has an abundant life for each of us." It's rarer to hear *how* the Enemy works in the particularity of our stories or *how* we can experience this abundant life. Instead what we often hear is "*Do* good and you'll *be* good." Don't get me wrong, I believe God does indeed have an abundant life for us. I also believe the Enemy is much more insidious than we want to believe. Where I find issue with some churches is their lack of invitation for people to honestly share their struggles and stories—not so they can be "fixed" with a prayer or a quick Scripture, but rather so they can have a safe space to process their trauma and pain, a space where they are welcomed with their doubts and questions and hurt, and are seen as people to be loved and not projects to be fixed. When spaces like this exist, the Holy Spirit is able to heal and redeem, and people can step back into who they were created to be—and experience truly abundant life.

The fully alive life isn't achieved by *doing* what you think is right; it's achieved by understanding and *being* who God created you to be. Behavior modifications can only drive us to other behaviors, which perpetuates a cycle of keeping God out of the fragile places of our heart. We play a game that goes against the truth that we have a God who sees us and loves us and invites us to partner with him in the adventure of life. We trade that amazing reality for the façade of being seen as put-together, polished, and perfect.

Maybe you're thinking none of this sounds like you. I mean, you are at the top of your game, really "killing it for the kingdom" kind of stuff. If this is you today, take a moment and look deep within yourself. If there are good parts of you that you have had to abandon or betray to be where you are today, then dear friend, there are parts of you that are not fully alive. These are the places that God wants to renew within you. There is freedom for you too; none of us have completed our sanctification process. The process to become more like Jesus is a journey, not a destination, so there is always more for him to heal within you.

The journey I'm inviting you into is for the brave, for the ones who are ready for a wild adventure. I'm asking you to be courageously honest about some of the strongly held beliefs you have about yourself. These beliefs may feel truer than the color of your eyes or the size of your feet. Some places inside you may have been covered up for so long that you almost forgot they were there—almost. God is not interested in your behavior change if leaving one behavior only leads you to adopt another behavior without undergoing real transformation (though he does want you to turn from the behaviors that bring harm and become idols that steal your heart). Transformation takes time. It takes honesty and surrender and courage. You will have to face and then die to some things that you know bring harm even though they have felt like friends. This will take a massive amount of courage.

But here's what I believe about you. You are strong, so strong. What you have seen and overcome has sometimes surprised you. I believe you can taste the goodness of the abundant life God offers, and you hunger for it. I believe when the lights are out and no one is around, you are caught between hope that propels you to dream and fear that keeps you stuck. I believe you are tenacious and good. In your heart, you just want to be fully known—even if that means someone has to see it all— because you hear a voice beckoning to you, offering the promise of becoming fully alive.

There is a way to experience this promise, but it's not found on the well-worn path of checking boxes and praying rehearsed prayers. It's found in a journey to encounter a God who wants you to shine, who has purpose written through the pages of your story, who knows it all and sees it all and still wants to bring about beauty through you. I have tried all the avenues and I'm no expert, but I am a testament of what it looks like to set down my religion (doing) and pick up a relationship (being) with a Father who cries with me, laughs with me, holds me, and calls me to dream. I have gone down many roads trying to find him, trying to make sense of the madness of my life. Where I found him most tangibly was in the honest places of my pain. There he was, preparing a banquet for me in the presence of my enemies, showing me tenderness in my moments of hatred and shame. When I tried to run and hide from my pain, it only continued the cycle, but he kept calling and reassuring me that even in grief, reality, and pain, I was safe, and there was hope.

Instead of providing a guided prayer to close this chapter, I encourage you to pray whatever is on your heart. Perhaps even write it in a journal so you can one day look back and see how far God has brought you. Share with him your hesitations and your excitements. Offer commitments about the work you plan to do, and be honest about the roadblocks you anticipate. Allow time to ponder what you've read and listen to what your heart is saying. Write what you sense the Lord is laying on your heart, even if it seems silly or doesn't make sense. Perhaps it's a memory, a picture, a word, or a sentence. Use this time to declare before yourself and the Lord what you want and what you need. You do not begin the journey alone. *He is with you.*

> So Jesus said to the Jews who had believed him, "If you abide
> in my word, you are truly my disciples, and you will know
> the truth, and the truth will set you free."
>
> **—John 8:31-32 (ESV)**

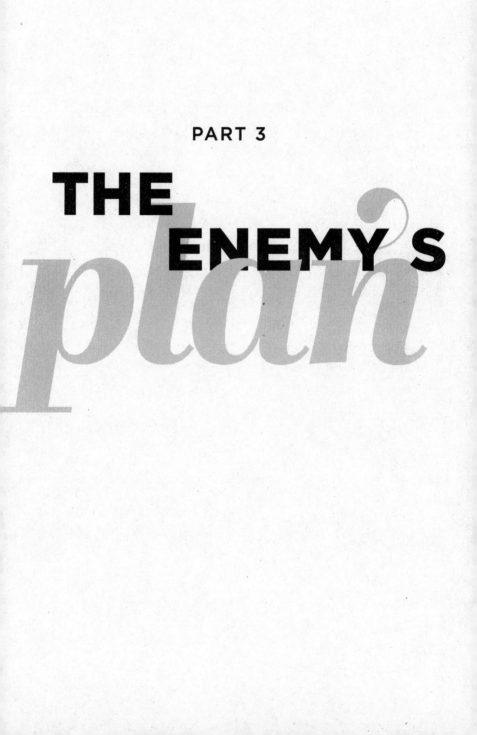

PART 3

THE ENEMY'S *plan*

CHAPTER 7

THE TRUTH OF THE ENEMY

I hate everything scary. Scary movies, scary commercials . . . I just hate being scared. My sister Shara, on the other hand, *loves* scary stuff. She watches all those crime shows and horror movies, and she loves a good haunted house. Every Halloween, she and my other siblings go to the scariest one they can find, and they always try to get me to go. They want me to go because they know how freaked out I'll get. One year, my sister asked me at just the right moment—when my FOMO had kicked in— and I buckled. I reluctantly said yes—one of the worst yeses of my life.

We waited in line for hours, having paid an obscene amount of money to have people terrorize us. When we finally entered, I couldn't even open my eyes. Each room was more terrifying than the next. People were screaming and yelling, and the few times I did open my eyes, there were scary clowns and zombies. I clung so tightly to my sister's arm that I'm pretty sure she still has scars from where my fingernails dug into her skin. Eventually, I saw some light coming in from a door up ahead and knew we were almost done. I sighed in relief. We were in the home stretch. I opened my eyes slightly and immediately saw a crazed figure coming toward me. It was as if this chainsaw-wielding psycho-zombie-farmer thing recognized that I was the scaredy-cat, the weakest link in the group, and waited for his moment to pounce. I screamed, "Oh, heck, no!" and tried to get around the people in front of us to leave. But it was too late. The farmer-zombie caught up to me and held his running chainsaw up next to my head, and I crumpled to the ground in fear (yes, I know it didn't have a chain in it and couldn't actually hurt me, but there's no room for rational thought when you're a grown woman lying on the ground in the fetal position).

As I shouted, "You are not allowed to touch me!" to the creature, Shara grabbed my arm and tried to get me up and to the exit. But I couldn't move. I was frozen in fear. I lay there for what felt like hours (but was probably only a minute or two) until the zombie person decided they had tortured me enough and walked away. With the torment over, I collected my disheveled self and the little dignity I had left and walked up the stairs to the exit. When I finally made it out the door, stripped of my self-respect, Shara couldn't stop laughing. To this day, she considers this one of the funniest memories we have together. I can laugh at it now too, but man, when I was in that haunted house, it felt real. Logically I knew I wouldn't be harmed—I knew the actors didn't have any real power or real weapons, so I would leave fine—but in the moment, my brain forgot that truth and succumbed to what it was being fed in the moment: fear.

In my haunted house story, that awful zombie creature was

my villain. In the stories of our lives, the main villain is the Enemy. He is the ultimate terror who has come to steal, kill, and destroy—to keep us from walking in freedom and abundance. Before we can walk in freedom, we must first understand what, or who, has put us in bondage—and why.

As silly as my haunted house story is, I think we often believe places like that are the only places we'll find the Enemy working. We think we'll only encounter him if we use a Ouija board, watch scary movies, or read books with bad magic in them. If we do have an encounter with the forces of darkness, we buckle in fear, because we have never been taught how to fight back! The reality is that the Enemy's work is not usually as obvious as a haunted house or a scary movie. His ways are far craftier and more sinister. His greatest weapon is convincing us he doesn't exist—and that if he does, it's only in the really "bad" places.

I have been working as a professional life coach for over a decade, and during that time I have heard many stories of horrific trauma. Some people aren't even aware of what they have endured and try to convince me they don't have a story. But they realize something is preventing them from experiencing the abundance they read about in Scripture. The longer I do this work, the more I'm convinced that the work of the Enemy has gone unnamed and unchallenged in many people's lives for far too long. His lies wisp in the shadows of our minds, pitting us against ourselves, God, and others. We may not always be able to name it, but most of us sense that there is something off in our bodies and minds.

I don't want to minimize the reality that the Enemy *does* work in some of the more obvious ways—and I don't want to downplay his power. He works covertly and overtly, and he is always at work. Therefore, it's important to understand how he may be working in our lives so we can combat his schemes and remind ourselves that though he is powerful, we are not his. We can say with full assuredness that we belong to God, and "the one who is in you is greater than the one who is in the world" (1 John 4:4).

Now listen—no one *wants* to talk about the Enemy. No one wants to dwell on the negatives of their life; we're tempted to move on and not reflect on the pain points. But stepping into the freedom we desire and the calling God has for us requires learning about the adversary who is fighting against us. Our purpose in this learning is not to fixate on him and let thoughts of him consume us, but rather to claim authority over him so we can walk in freedom. Once we have exposed his tactics and his lies, we will be able to take our harmful thoughts—the lies we've accepted through the Enemy's schemes—captive with authority and truth.

It's common to feel powerless against the Enemy's attacks; many people have never learned how personalized these attacks can be. Often people experience attacks early in life in the places they're uniquely gifted, because the Enemy will stop at nothing to dim the light of God's creation. Boys with sensitive hearts are mocked by their fathers for being too soft, or humiliated on the playground for being weak, and they grow into men who believe the lie that their soft heart is a liability and they'd better not show it. Girls with bold ideas and vision are attacked into second-guessing everything they do for fear of being rejected or looking stupid. I've heard women tell stories about how their mother would give a look of embarrassment that said, "You are too much for me," or how church congregants would take Scriptures out of context to teach that women were to be silent and not talk. People's wounds often line up with the very gifts and purposes God has given them. This story has been repeated throughout history—after all, if the enemy attacked Jesus so personally in the desert, tempting him in the very areas that were linked to his power and position, could it be possible that this is how the Enemy works with us too?

While the Enemy is not mentioned often in Scripture, we can see his hand at work throughout—from Abraham taking matters into his own hands, to Peter denying Jesus out of fear, to Judas betraying him for power and position. The Enemy will often attack where we are gifted and called. It's as if he sees the potential God has placed in us and wants to eradicate it. If he can't kill us, he will do everything in his power to distract and discourage us. Abraham was discouraged by the waiting time required to step into the fullness of his calling, so he tried to rush things along and brought only further heartache and destruction (Genesis 16). Peter was a gifted, powerful speaker, but fear crept in and silenced his voice, leading him to deny knowing Jesus (Luke 22:54–62). Judas had a trusted role as treasurer, indicating that this was one of his giftings. However, even while he was under the teachings of Jesus, Judas became an embezzler, enticed by greed under the devil's influence (John 12:6).

The Enemy discourages and distracts us so he can use our gifting in a way that causes destruction. Our talents often become the places he attacks most severely. He sees the gifting and wants to twist it and use it for his gain. These attacks lead to trauma in our stories; seemingly small experiences collide to form an overall narrative woven through our life.

His attacks occur in stories like the boy who didn't make the baseball team, and when he came home to tell his mom, she looked at him with disappointment and walked out of the room. In that moment, the whisper began: "You're a disappointment, and love will leave if you don't perform better."

Or the young girl who stood on the playground and lost herself in her imagination only to realize she was being mocked by the cool girls because she was "weird" and "different." The whisper began: "Your imagination is a liability; stop dreaming, because it's made you a fool."

Or the teen who was full of life and energy but soon realized her body did not match up to others', and the ridicule she faced for being chubby was more than she could bear. The whisper began: "If you don't get a better body, you'll never find love or be accepted. Control your urges to eat."

Or the husband whose wife had an affair, leaving him feeling emasculated and alone. The whisper began: "Turn on your computer. You will find satisfaction through the screen."

Or the young girl whose personality was larger than life but who felt the jealousy of a mom who couldn't stand her goodness because of her own brokenness. The whisper began: "Dim your light or you'll lose your mom's affection."

The list could go on and on, because these are real stories and these are the whispers that grow in the background. The Enemy will assault the sensitive heart, the bright and shining star, the dreamer, or the entrepreneur. I think many of us have this idea that the bad guy is running around trying to scare us and possess us, but he usually operates more slyly than that. Fear is his tactic, and he launches his assault by creating fear that you won't belong if you are truly who you were created to be. He begins by convincing you that something about you is genuinely flawed. You then feel shame, which makes you want to stay far away from God, fearing that the gifts he gave you will make you subject to betrayal, abandonment, or rejection. The Enemy studies your story, he watches where you light up the room and where your unique design brings delight to the world, and that's what he attacks. His assault is specific to you, and he has been studying you for years.

At this point, you may want to throw the book across the room. Instead, let this section open your eyes so you can know the truth and be set free from the lies that have kept you bound! With this knowledge, you can finally take back what the Enemy has stolen. Evil hates what is good, and the Enemy knows that you bear goodness because you were created in the image of God. The Enemy is hell-bent on getting you to walk away from that goodness. A silenced and beat-down child of God is no threat to his kingdom—but God won't let him have the final word in your story.

Looking deeper into your story will help you see how the Enemy tries to keep you as far as possible from the person God created you to be. This plan has been going on since you were little, focusing its attack on your particular gifting. The Enemy knows you're a threat to the kingdom of darkness. He knows that if you choose to really read this chapter, along with the Scriptures mentioned, he will be no match for what Jesus can do in you. Then he will be forced to flee, and the calling you have been wanting to step into will emerge.

In Ephesians 6:11 (ESV), Paul tells us to "put on the whole armor of God, that you may be able to stand against the schemes of the devil." In the next verse, he tells us that "we do not wrestle against flesh and blood, but against the rulers, against the authorities, against the cosmic powers over this present darkness, against the spiritual forces of evil in the heavenly places." He goes on to tell us how to combat the schemes of the Enemy. We do not use weapons of this world, but we have been given authority over the lies that try to destroy us. When we put on the full armor of God, we are able to defend ourselves against the lies that come at us; when we know the truth of God's Word, we can begin to sift through what is true and what is not. The greatest weapon we have is prayer. My grandpa used to say, "Where prayer is focused, power falls." God does not leave us lacking. However, we must do the work of making sure we are covered and seeking him for help in the areas of our lives that are being attacked. If we think any of us will skate by without experiencing a full-blown assault because of whose image we are made in, we will be truly disillusioned by this life.

What God created in perfection, the Enemy has come to destroy. His main goal is to disconnect you from the Father, to plant seeds of doubt and shame, and to use harm inflicted on you by others to spin a narrative that keeps you bound to his lies. His approach is beyond crafty; it's focused on the very places of your calling. If he can get you separated from who God created you to be, if he can get you to doubt the goodness of God, and if he can isolate you from others, he has successfully silenced a child who was designed for immeasurable influence within the kingdom of God. The Enemy's plan is calculated and insidious, and he has been working within the pages of your story for years.

Dear Lord, protect me from the Enemy. As I learn of his wicked ways, show me how to use the authority you've given me to win the battle against him. Reveal his lies to me so that they no longer have power over me or my story, and empower me as I put on the full armor of God. In Jesus's name, amen.

CHAPTER 8

THE THIEF, THE MURDERER, AND THE DESTROYER

To better understand how the Enemy works in the particularities of your story, let's break down John 10:10: "The thief comes only to steal and kill and destroy" (ESV). This verse appears in the context of a passage about how deeply a shepherd cares for his sheep. Without a good shepherd watching over them, the sheep are vulnerable to attack. A wolf may come along and snatch some of the sheep, causing the flock to scatter in fear and confusion. In this story, Jesus is the shepherd, we are the sheep, and the Enemy is the wolf. He comes to steal, kill, and destroy by separating us from the shepherd. But what does this look like in our lives?

The Enemy Is a Thief

The Enemy steals our innocence. He can take away play, the desire to create, and the beauty of an imagination connected to God. When you are a child, you don't have the logic necessary to fight against lies that are whispered to you. Also, we're all raised by flawed people—and the Enemy seizes this as an opportunity, using the very people who are supposed to be safe to play into his assault. It's hard to acknowledge, I know. But the truth is we *all* have had our parents, teachers, siblings, loved ones, and others let us down. When this happens, the Enemy jumps right in, and the whispers begin. When you are little, you have no defenses. Your primary goal as a child is to have a sense of belonging and not to lose love. So you adjust and silence the parts of you that make you different and threaten that sense of belonging and longing for love. This is how innocence is stolen.

Jesus is very clear that he loves children. He expresses how highly he regards them and calls us to be more like them (Matthew 18:1–5). He even issues a warning that if anyone causes a child to stumble, "it would be better for them to have a large millstone hung around their neck and to be drowned in the depths of the sea" (Matthew 18:6). Whoa! Jesus is letting the disciples know that we are to highly regard and protect the ones who are seemingly insignificant—the young, who are subject to all kinds of attacks. We are to be his watchful eyes and ears, alert to the ploy of the Enemy against these young hearts.

The Enemy waits to pounce, looking for moments and people he can use to steal the innocence from our stories. He steals play and imagination, leaving behind only cynicism and distrust. Look around. What do you see happening in our world? Our children are being targeted. This is not by coincidence. The Enemy is smart and crafty and knows that if he can get his talons into people when they're young, without someone exposing him, he'll have them for life.

We can't bury our heads in the sand. We must open our eyes to the work the Enemy is doing, both inside us and around us. That's why this "story work"—that is, reflecting on how the Enemy has whispered lies to us throughout our lives so we can refute those lies and walk freely and fully alive in the calling God has for us—is so important. When the Enemy shuts down our sense of play and our childlike innocence, he shuts down our freedom and keeps us in bondage to the twisted lies he has whispered over us. If we don't expose the truth of what he's stolen from us, we will go on living in bondage to him for a lifetime—even if we know all the Scripture and pray all the prayers. We must break our unknowing agreements with the Enemy, with the power of Christ as our authority.

The Enemy Is a Killer

Most of us have an internal gauge that helps us fight off the kind of deep hopelessness that leads some people to take their own lives, but the numbers are not looking good for our society. According to the National Center for Health Statistics, the suicide rate increased 30 percent from 2000 to 2020; suicide is the twelfth leading cause of death in the United States.[1]

Death is the goal of the Enemy, and he seems to be gaining ground.

God created our bodies with the garden of Eden in mind.

The fullness of humanity in all its original perfection was sown into the garden at its creation. When Satan invaded the sanctity of Eden and sin entered the world through temptation and deception, humanity's desires became twisted. Hearts that had been marked by purity, goodness, and desire fueled by perfect peace became desperate hearts at war with the flesh.

We know this did not come from God, because James 1:13–15 tells us, "When tempted, no one should say, 'God is tempting me.' For God cannot be tempted by evil, nor does he tempt anyone; but each person is tempted when they are dragged away by their own evil desire and enticed. Then, after desire has conceived, it gives birth to sin; and sin, when it is full-grown, gives birth to death." So, my friends, don't be fooled by your own desires!

James was speaking of the post-fall disordered desires of the flesh. Eve was enticed by an Enemy who played upon her curiosity (remember, at this point, she had no sin within her) and fed into her natural desires for food, beauty, and to be like God. The consequence was the entrance of sin into the world; humans would now experience an inner war between their desire for goodness and their shadow side of perversion. Adam and Eve, who were once innocent, became riddled with shame. They looked upon their bodies and instantly felt the sting of death and perversion.

The tactics Satan used with Eve are the same ones he uses today. He wants to kill the God-given desires within you or pervert those desires into "the lust of the flesh, the lust of the eyes, and the pride of life" (1 John 2:16 NKJV). He takes what you were created for and twists it. The very places you were meant to bring delight end up being places where you self-sabotage or sabotage others.

My husband, Mario, is a great listener. He brings peace to most situations, and he has a tender heart toward people who have been abused and neglected. When I first met Mario, he hadn't yet done the work to know where the Enemy had assaulted him. I believe Mario was created to offer a caring ear and an empathetic heart, but without healing, he instead shut people out, and his presence became cold and unengaged. The very thing he was created to do was the very thing he would withhold, because he didn't understand the shame cycle he was in. This cycle was fed by a narrative that told him his softness and empathetic heart would lead to pain and expose him as weak and unfit to be a husband, dad, or friend. He wanted to be who he knew he could be, but he'd had many experiences that made him believe the lie that it would be better if he were quiet and closed off, so he shrank into a version of himself that played right into the Enemy's strategy.

When our desires become disordered, it's not because we want to be broken and isolated from God and others; rather, we're driven by our untended-to stories. Our experiences of harm affect how we see ourselves, God, and others. The temptation to sin speaks to the parts of us that long to be loved unconditionally and accepted as we are, and to have the depths of our hearts known and not rejected. When your heart has not been tended to and you couple that with the sinful desires of the flesh, you are no match for the schemes of the Enemy on your own. Surrendering your story to the kindness and care of the Lord can reorder your desires and allow for flourishing to happen and for Eden-like moments to come back to you, on earth as it is in heaven.

Satan's plan for the world is for humanity to be destroyed. He knows he does not have the power to do that, though, so he will try every tactic in the book to relegate the people of God to the shadows, all the while whispering lies that keep us bound to the agreements and strongholds that have been placed over us. He will offer counterfeit ways to fulfill your desire to be known and loved, while keeping you distracted from the truth of who God has created you to be, the power you hold, and God's unshakable love for you. Satan's temptations satiate your longings for a moment but then leave you in a cycle of shame and addiction. He may not kill your physical body, but if he can kill your desire to bring goodness to the land of the living, he has taken you out of the fight and you are now no threat to him.

We must fight back. We must take back what is rightfully ours. You don't have to settle for a slow death according to the Enemy's plan.

The Enemy Destroys

To destroy is to deform and mar, to ruin something and keep it from its original intent. How do we see the Enemy trying to deform or mar us in our stories? Envision a hand. A hand is meant to hold, to carry, to grip and to grab. If that hand is injured so severely that its mobility is affected, then the hand has been rendered useless and can no longer fulfill its original purpose. The deformation happens because something has gone awry; the hand was originally created to function as a hand. Without restoration and healing, the hand will never regain the function for which it was created.

The Enemy works in this same way with the lies he tells.

He desires to make you believe so many lies about yourself that you can't even remember your dreams or desires. He wants you to stop believing you have gifts and talents, so that you won't be able to help but operate in fear, isolation, and doubt. He makes you turn on yourself, heaping shame upon you with accusatory words like "stupid," "liar," and "dumb." He makes you believe that if you reveal your true heart, you will be rejected and mocked. He takes your intended purpose and twists the longings of your heart, leaving you feeling destroyed and deformed, no longer fit for any good use.

Scripture gives us many warnings about being alert to the schemes of the Enemy: "Be alert and of sober mind. Your enemy the devil prowls around like a roaring lion looking for someone to devour" (1 Peter 5:8). But we can do more than be on the defense against the Enemy. If we know how he operates, we can also have an offensive plan to see through his lies and walk in freedom.

Temptation will always be present in our lives, especially as we get closer to our original design—who God created us to be. With eyes open to the truth and a heart surrendered to God, you now have a choice. The love of the Father will draw you closer to him and further from the Enemy who has had a hold on you for so long. You will not fall prey to the devil's antics or seek your own pleasure or desires; pursuing the will of God will empower you and bring freedom:

> Delight yourself in the LORD,
>   and he will give you the *desires* of your heart.
>
> **—Psalm 37:4 (ESV, emphasis added)**

Dear Lord, please keep me alert to the schemes of the Enemy. Keep my mind sober and strong against temptation. Renew the innocence that has been stolen from me, and renew my confidence in who you created me to be. In Jesus's name, amen.

CHAPTER 9

SUIT UP AND FIGHT

Whether you acknowledge it or not, there is a battle waging all around us. You can pretend it's not happening and cross your fingers and hope it gets better, or you can suit up and fight. When you fight with the authority of Christ, the Enemy has to flee. And understanding how the Enemy works within the particularities of your story will help you launch your counterattack with precision.

There are two places in Scripture where we see Satan tempt through dialogue. The first is with Eve in the garden, and the second is when Jesus was tempted in the wilderness. Satan used the same tactics in both instances, but he also appealed to the particularities of their potential fleshly desires. As we know, one of these people succumbed to the temptation (Eve), and one did not (Jesus). One chose to stand on the truth, and the other did not. If we want to know how to win in a spiritual battle, we must know how Satan fights.

He has had the same playbook since the very first moment he wielded his crafty ways in Genesis 3—and he still uses the same tactics today! First, he isolates. What's the first thing he did in Genesis? He got Eve alone. This isolation allowed him to say whatever he wanted to her without another person chiming in and challenging him. Second, he made her question what she heard from God, which produced doubt. By using the phrase "Did God really say . . .", Satan left Eve second-guessing what she had heard and wondering whether God really was good if he was keeping something from her. Third, he made her question her identity ("For God knows that when you eat from [the tree] . . . you will be like God, knowing good and evil"). This led to chaos as she stepped away from the wholeness of who she was created to be.

It's in these three places—isolation, doubt, and chaos—that the Enemy works. And as we read earlier in James, there is a process to temptation. Think about the internal dialogue that gives birth to sin and then in turn gives birth to death (James 1:15). We often follow a progression of three lies to justify our sin: "This won't hurt me." "I need this to be fulfilled." "I can control this behavior." We see it with Eve in the garden, and we see it in our own lives. The Enemy's trap is set, and we are all too quick to step in it.

I often saw the Enemy's use of isolation to trap people in shame and sin when I worked in youth ministry. Students would come and be on fire for Jesus. They would praise and play and volunteer. Then one or two of them would stop coming to gatherings and not return phone calls, seeming to have fallen off the face of the earth. When I would finally get a hold of them, they would tell me how terrible they thought they were for mistakes they had made; they would say they needed to "get their life right" before coming back. This is a vicious cycle. Temptation happens, we stay silent about the temptation or sin, we eventually fall prey to it, and then we are ensnared by the shame of having fallen into it. We are often no different from those students; we too get caught up in thoughts like "If anyone knew this, they wouldn't want to know me." Our minds become isolated from truth, doubt sets in, and the chaos of not knowing who we are in this world destroys us—we forget "that we are of God, and the whole world lies under the sway of the wicked one" (1 John 5:19 NKJV).

The Enemy exerts his sway in this world by tempting us with "the lust of the flesh, the lust of the eyes, and the pride of life" (1 John 2:16 NKJV). Knowing how the Enemy operates, we can look to Scripture to see how Jesus modeled what we can do to combat these attacks on our lives. In Matthew 4 we find Jesus fasting in the wilderness for forty days. At the end of his fast he found himself face-to-face with the devil himself. Jesus was fully man, so he was tired, hungry, and feeling alone. The devil used this vulnerability to try to make Jesus doubt God by twisting the words of God and trying to assault Jesus's identity. We can see Satan's tactics clear as day. He uses these same tactics thousands of years later, and yet we still fall prey.

But we don't have to anymore. As we read Matthew 4, we see how Jesus was tempted by his physical needs, the lust of the flesh, when the devil tempted him to turn stones to bread. But instead of succumbing to the flesh, Jesus recited the Scripture that speaks to the truth that people need far more than just bread to survive; they depend on every word that comes from the mouth of God (verse 4). Jesus was then tempted to jump off the highest point of the temple and demonstrate his deity through the angels who would come to rescue him—here we see the potential for Jesus to be tempted by the lust of the eyes. But instead of giving in to the temptation for all men to see his majesty in this moment, Jesus stated, "It is also written: 'Do not put the Lord your God to the test'" (verse 7). Finally, Jesus was offered all the kingdoms of the world if he would worship Satan, thereby giving in to the pride of life. This is the moment when Jesus, in his authority, commanded Satan to leave and claimed the truth of Scripture by reciting the words "Worship the Lord your God, and serve him only" (verse 10). Jesus used three powerful tactics to combat the Enemy. First, Jesus used the truth of Scripture. He denied his feelings of hunger and held to truth. Second, he responded with specificity. He did not just use random Scriptures; he chose specific verses to respond to the devil's specific temptations. This demonstrates how we must fight off temptation in the particularities of how it comes. Third, Jesus cast the Enemy out. He did not have his Father in heaven do this; he exercised his own authority to bind and throw out the Enemy. This is a key point. We often ask God to take away our temptation when God has given *us* the authority. We're the ones who made our "contracts and agreements" with the Enemy, so it's up to us to break them with the power of Jesus Christ. We get to stand firm, and the Enemy must flee. He will continue to try to attack, but we can stand firm, ready to fight with truth and specificity, ultimately binding him in the name of Jesus Christ.

> *Dear Lord, teach me how to stand firm when the Enemy tempts me. Protect me from his lies and give me the power and courage to break the contracts I have made—intentionally and unintentionally—with him throughout my life so I can walk in the calling you have for me. In Jesus's name, amen.*

PART 4

CONNECTION TO
self

CHAPTER 10

EMOTIONAL LANGUAGE

Years ago, I was hanging with my stepmom, Kimberly. We were pulling into her driveway after running errands, and before I got out of the car, she said, "Karrie, I'd like to speak to your heart about something."

Now, you need to know something about Kimberly. Whenever she says these words, you know something big is coming. The words always come with a smile, but that smile is only there to ease the blow of what you're about to hear. I was in my thirties at the time, and my kids were little. Kimberly hadn't been married to my dad for that long, so what she was about to say took an incredible amount of bravery and risk. She looked me in the eyes and spoke straight to my shame. With kindness, she spoke to me about my anger, how it was affecting my kids, and how it was affecting me. She told me I was a good mom, but my anger was hurting my kids' spirits. Friend, I wept. It was the kind of weeping where you can't catch your breath. It was beyond painful. I had been in therapy for years and had been doing the work—I thought I had overcome my anger problem! Because of that, Kimberly's words seriously caught me off guard.

But within moments, I knew she was right. I left the car feeling the weight of our conversation and went inside to lie down. I wept and thought of how I wanted so much more for my kids than what I had experienced growing up. They deserved a mom who was free of this burden. But I couldn't will away my propensity for anger, and although therapy seemed to be helping, it was clear that I was still bound to this rage.

In that moment, I wept for myself. My anger was my reality, but I had missed the root of why it was there. God dropped a question on my heart: "What is making you sad? If you press past the shame of being angry, what do you find?" "Longing," I said. As he asked me what I was longing for, I realized that I wished my mom could have been around to be the one to confront me about my shortcomings as a mom. I wished she could have taught me how to be a better mom and nurtured me with love and care as Kimberly did. I knew I needed to continue the work of dealing with my anger, but what I discovered in that moment is that God wanted to uncover a much deeper grief.

What I was feeling in that moment was not shame or guilt; it was grief. I needed to be comforted. Acknowledging that need allowed God to enter the places of deep longing in my heart. The bigger truth of the story is that my mom was never the nurturing mom I desired when she was alive. Because of this, I had created a narrative that said I didn't need anyone to help me, and this narrative felt like truth to me. "You don't need anyone, Karrie; you are strong on your own." In fact, my role in this narrative was to be the rescuer of those who were in need. If I couldn't save my mom, then I could save the world. Can you imagine the burden of that narrative? The impossible expectation? I wasn't an angry person because I wanted to be angry; I was an angry person because I was wounded, and anger helped me to stay safe by keeping people and love at a distance.

In the years since my conversation with Kimberly, I have spent many hours unpacking my story and the emotions I carry. As someone who has struggled with anger, depression, anxiety, and imposter syndrome, I can say with full assurance that there is no way to avoid pain in your journey toward living fully alive. Trust me, I've tried. I may have made huge advances at times, but I've also inevitably gone right back into cycles of false freedom.

When we engage the painful parts of our stories, it's crucial that we name what we were feeling in those moments, as well as the emotions we feel today when we think back on them. Perhaps you feel anger when you think about a failed relationship—but what is behind that anger? Are you feeling grief over the loss of where you thought that relationship would go? Do you feel betrayed? Did someone violate your trust? To revisit these stories and identify what was going on in your heart, it is important to understand *emotional language*. Emotional language is the ability to give words to what you are feeling. For many of us, it is hard to know what we are feeling and why; putting words to our feelings helps us better express what is going on inside our hearts, which allows us to experience deeper connection with ourselves, God, and others.

For many years I believed the lie that God would think more of me if I pretended I was okay. This belief may seem ridiculous since God sees all things—yet how often do we pretend with God? You know, "Fake it till ya make it!" When we are upset, lost, or hurting, we often ignore or mask our true feelings, expecting that God will just take them away. We avoid having an honest conversation with our loving Father and inviting him into our pain. This was me for so long. Instead of crying out to God, I pretended I was fine, listened for my marching orders from him, and continued to follow the call I believed he had for me. I ignored all the times in Scripture when God's people cried out and he listened and drew near to them.

The truth is that God created us to be emotional—and he promises to meet us in our heavy emotions. Matthew 5:4 tells us, "Blessed are those who mourn, for they will be comforted." Mourning leads to blessing in the form of a promise of comfort. When we avoid our emotions, we miss out on the comfort of a loving Father and on the blessing that will come from being honest about our grief.

We must apply emotional language and welcome the voices of our present and our past to help us escape the snares of our past. Emotions are the "check engine" light on our body's proverbial dashboard. They were never intended to drive our decision-making; they are the helpers that call attention to the issues going on inside us. As such, we must not ignore them, but we also must not indulge in them too much. When we ignore our emotions, we deny what our body needs, and we deny God access to the places of our heart that need care. The flip side is allowing emotions to dictate our behaviors and beliefs, which also inevitably keeps Jesus far from our wounds. Both approaches are coping mechanisms to avoid sitting in our pain, and both will keep us from moving into true transformation.

> The purposes of a person's heart are deep waters,
>   but one who has insight draws them out.
>
> **—Proverbs 20:5**

When I looked beneath the shame of being an angry mom who was crushing her kids' spirits, I saw that I was holding on to the grief of not having had a caring mom myself. In a similar way, you can identify your emotions and then pray for God to help you identify your deeper pain and longing.

As you begin the work of identifying your emotions and understanding how they affect you, I invite you to envision your feelings as an iceberg. Or, if your imagination is taking the day off, just look at the following illustration.

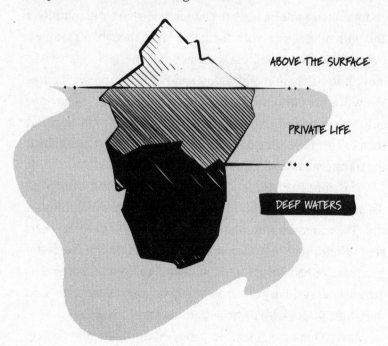

ABOVE THE SURFACE

PRIVATE LIFE

DEEP WATERS

The top layer of the iceberg is "above the surface"—the feelings you have that can be seen by all. The actions and emotions that appear at this level have all come from deeper emotions in the layers below; they are the outcomes of deeper waters. But at the top is what everyone sees—your happy, sad, and angry emotions. It's also where your coping behaviors exist, keeping you from feeling what is deeper.

The second layer of the iceberg is your private life. Maybe people close to you know about the more personal areas of your life, or maybe they are known only by you. I call this level the "seen, but not known" level. This is the level at which our church, small group, accountability partners, and maybe even spouses tend to know us. Being known at this level is good, and it's often as deep as we're comfortable going with ourselves and with others. The truth about this layer, though, is that if we stop here and only address the emotions on this level, we will move into behavior modification and not heart transformation. We will spin our wheels, trying to stop our "bad" behaviors, only to move to other behaviors to try to mitigate our hurt and shame. This may bring relief for a while, but it won't bring about the transformation we desire.

The third layer of the iceberg is the deep waters—the place where secrets and trauma live, and where God wants to comfort you. The memories and emotions that exist in our deepest waters are the ones that have had profound impact on our lives—for good and for bad. When we allow ourselves to enter this level by getting honest about our deeper emotions and then inviting God into those places with us, true transformation begins.

As a young mom, I seemed happy on my "above the surface" level. Kimberly saw beyond that, into the "private life" level of anger I was holding. But what was going on in my deepest waters was a desire to have had a mom who cared for me and exemplified the mom I was trying to be.

It may feel daunting to consider diving into your deep internal waters. Perhaps your waters are filled with trauma that you don't want to relive. I understand that. If that's you, I encourage you to take this process one step at a time. Be kind to yourself as you journey back into your story, and ask God to stay near and comfort you along the way. When a new or unfamiliar emotion comes up, ask yourself, "What am I thinking right now, and what do I feel about that thought?" Then ask yourself, "What do I need in this moment?" and ask God to meet that need. Don't try to rush through your emotions or get frustrated when you can't "get over" something quickly; your emotions are signaling a deeper need that God wants to address.

Remember, God gave us feelings as indicators of all that is going on inside us. And though emotions aren't intended to drive our decisions, I have learned that when I don't honor my emotions, I miss my deep needs—which ultimately does end up driving my actions. This doesn't just apply to negative emotions either. When we don't have emotional language, we shut off all emotions—including joy, peace, and love. Stuffing bad emotions turns into ignoring good ones, and this leaves us completely cut off from what is really going on in our deep waters—causing a disconnect in how we see God, ourselves, and others.

Learning to identify and name your emotions may not come easily to you—and that is completely fine. And even if you *think* you're good at it, you may be surprised to find that what you are feeling in a given moment is actually the manifestation of a deeper, different emotion. As you begin learning to identify your emotions so you can meet the needs each emotion requires, you may find it helpful to look online for lists of emotions. There are plenty out there that will help you expand your emotional language. Be kind to yourself in the process; many of us have not been taught this kind of language or shown the value of identifying our hurt.

> *Dear Lord, help me to understand my own heart. Help me see that engaging my emotions won't drown me; rather, avoiding them will. You have given me emotions to help heal me and to move me into deeper relationships with those I love, including you. Give me wisdom to see the underlying longings I carry, and give me the courage to sit with those longings and bring them before you. In Jesus's name, amen.*

CHAPTER 11

THE "T" WORD

What comes to your mind when you think of the term *trauma*? Does it make you think of abuse or sexual assault? Maybe you think of a physical trauma, like a car accident. For many of us, the term implies a big, scary, that-didn't-happen-to-me scenario. We think traumas are something *other* people experience. Maybe you have experienced many challenging moments in your life but would never call them traumas. Regardless of what you've thought about trauma in the past, let's create a shared definition as we journey together toward freedom and living fully alive. A trauma, in layman's terms, is any circumstance in which a person feels powerless; a fracture occurs, and an imprint of loss or pain is left behind. In some cases, this lack of power—whether caused by a person or situation—impresses itself so deeply that the effects are felt years or even decades later. If you've ever been to therapy, it's likely that you've addressed some of your traumas or spent time trying to identify traumas in your life. We've discussed the roots of our pain in previous chapters, and those roots are often tied to a trauma—or a need that resulted from that trauma.

Our brains tend to default to survival mode; we try to avoid experiencing the pain of trauma at all costs. I think our bodies, minds, and spirits are always longing to get back to the peace of Eden. Jewish people refer to a deep sense of peace as *shalom,* which means completeness or wholeness. We were made for Eden and our spirits crave heaven, so we will do anything we can to try to keep a sense of shalom in our hearts in the in-between.

To understand trauma is to understand sin, brokenness, and our desperate needs. To ignore trauma is to deny sin and its power over us. When we come to Christ, we gain power over sin, but there's a very real learning curve when it comes to stepping into that power, and we often leave our traumas unaddressed in the meantime—which means trauma has time to make its mark. This leads to shame, which is never from God. When we are in a place of shame, like Adam and Eve after they ate the fruit, we want to hide from God because we are ashamed that we fell into the traps and lies set before us. We were deceived by the Enemy, yet he manages to flip the script so we believe it was all our fault. In our minds, we are the terrible ones, but this is a lie the Enemy speaks over us. This is how shame begins to have its way.

Trauma and abuse therapist (and my professor) Dr. Dan Allender teaches about experiencing shalom in our hearts. He states that we are born with a sense of shalom, but that shalom is shattered when we experience pain or trauma. In that shattering we make agreements with the Enemy that cause us to believe that the only way to experience love and acceptance is to cover up who we are. (Dr. Allender explains this much better than I can. I highly encourage you to read his books, listen to his podcast, or consider attending a workshop if you're interested in learning more about this.)

How many times has shalom been shattered throughout our stories, even in small ways, and somehow resulted in our making agreements with the Enemy about our identities? How was my mom's shalom shattered, and how did that affect her? I will never fully understand the traumas my mom experienced as a child that led to her feeling isolated and desperate for acceptance. What I do know, though, is that those painful moments shattered my mom's shalom, and she made agreements with the Enemy that she would hide her pain with outward beauty, being skinny, and being the "perfect" pastor's wife. Unfortunately, this only masked her pain and bred intense shame. She did everything she could to make sure no one ever saw what was really going on in her heart.

This is how the Enemy works: he takes moments of our lives and twists them to make sure we never show up as our true selves but instead hide parts of ourselves. He wants us to believe we won't be loved if we are our true selves, the selves God created us to be. These lies build up over time, and before we know it, all of who we were created to be is in some type of hiding. Our unchecked trauma-filled moments then build up and, without good care around them, they create in us a sense of shame as they did for my mom. This shame is where the Enemy does his best

work. As you can see in the diagram, unchecked shame leads to hate or disgust—either toward yourself or toward others—and that hate becomes the way you deal with your shame.

The trauma diagram gives us a simple way of understanding trauma, which we've defined as any time we've experienced powerlessness that was not tended to well. In these times, empathy and kindness and good care were desperately needed but not received. Maybe your best friend moved away when you were little, and your parents told you, "Don't cry; you'll make new friends." So, you "moved on" and never grieved that loss. Or maybe a trusted friend did something horrible to you, and you never told anyone because you didn't want to mar that person's reputation. So, you "moved on" and never spoke about it. Whatever the circumstance, trauma creates a wound. If that wound isn't met with care, it becomes a scar, and that scar causes shame. If that shame isn't engaged and examined with kindness, you become filled with hate and disgust, whether directed at yourself or others. This is the goal of the Enemy—to keep you bound to hate, avoiding the shame, and never speaking of the trauma.

The beauty of this diagram is that it can help you identify your traumas so that you can engage with them, identify the care you never received, and then invite God into your need. This is how healing happens. The tough thing about identifying traumas is that they aren't always "big T" traumas that are easy to identify; they are often small imprints, whether they happened once or over time, that have become your truth. The first step in identifying these traumas is asking yourself, "What are the reasons why I hate myself or hate others?" Or if that sounds too harsh, try thinking about your self-talk instead. Are you constantly thinking things like "I'm stupid/disgusting/fat/ugly/annoying," or

"I'm not that pretty," or "My life would be better if it were more like that person's"? Negative self-talk is a clear indication of contempt for yourself. The same goes for your thoughts about others. Thoughts like "I don't need friends; I'm better off on my own," "I bet she paid for that perfect body," or "I'm sure his kids aren't this well-behaved at home" are all indications of

hate toward others. These types of thoughts are telltale signs that shame is at work and uncared-for traumas are present.

Stay with me here, friend. As you can see in the diagram above, we must work our way backward through our pain and hurt. Following your contempt (hate/disgust) with curiosity will lead you back to your shame. Curiosity is an offering of kindness to yourself. Ask yourself: "Why am I thinking such hateful words about myself? Why do some people's actions make me so angry?" Try to follow the thread of contempt back to a time you felt shame around that specific area.

Did you catch that? Your contempt is linked to a wound, and a wound not tended to well can lead to shame. When you engage your shame and identify your scars and wounds, you open the door to reveal the moment of trauma (the root cause of the shame and contempt). Once that trauma is identified, a new path appears: one where God can give new meaning to that moment and healing begins. Second Corinthians 10:5 says, "We demolish arguments and every pretension that sets itself up against the knowledge of God, and we take captive every thought to make it obedient to Christ." Thoughts are important, and they have more power over us than we care to admit. The beauty of this passage is that we have weapons to fight with. We have the power of the Holy Spirit to tear down strongholds of the Enemy, but we can't tear down the strongholds if we don't examine where they came from.

A few years ago I decided to take an inventory of my thoughts. I wrote down my negative self-talk whenever I had it, and after a week I had a pretty good list. Interestingly, my accusatory thoughts seemed to revolve around a few themes: "I'm too much for everyone." "I will never measure up." "I'm a terrible mom." The insidious voice of these lies was cruel and mocking and kept me stuck in my own head. After tracing the thoughts back through the shame and into the stories of trauma, I found they were all linked to some of my most wounding stories. Ironically, the lies that were torturing me ended up being (after God began to redeem my story) tied to the places of my gifting. I am larger than life; it's a gift to carry a room well. And I was never meant to measure up because I am, with Christ, enough, and my call is to help others realize that too. When I examined my thoughts and allowed God to reveal the deeper trauma stories, he began to redeem my story, and I began to see how the Enemy had attacked me in the first place. He *knew* that I held the glory of God and that glory can change the world!

Day after day, year after year, you may find yourself sitting in church doing all the things "required" to experience freedom. You do the Bible studies and read the books; you even volunteer in the children's ministry! You do these things out of an honest desire to learn and grow, but when the lights are out and no one is around, you lie in your room wondering if this is all there is. No matter what you do, you find yourself stuck, frustrated, numb, and maybe even angry. Working hard to leave your stories of trauma in the past won't free you from these stories. They are part of what makes you who you are. The trauma of those moments has affected you, and your body holds pain as a result. When we ignore our moments of trauma and fail to bring them into the light of day, where we could receive God's care and comfort, we stay bound to the pain they've caused us. The trauma becomes lodged in our bodies and begins to dictate how we love, lead, listen, and act.

Going back to uncover our trauma can be scary, and the process may seem confusing. This is where we get to rely on the Holy Spirit. He guides us to the places where we need healing. His whisper beckons us to unlock those places of our story and invite him in. The light of his presence shines upon the dark places of our heart, moving us past our shame and into the moments of trauma themselves, where he offers the comfort required for us to move into a new path, a new way of thinking, and an opportunity to heal. You don't have to live in bondage to your past anymore. There is a better way. Trauma will always be a part of our stories since we live in a fallen world, but the trauma of your story does not have to dictate how you live.

Bring your stories of trauma into God's light, and let the power of the Holy Spirit tend to those moments that have had far too much control over your life. Yes, this will require you to take courage and open the door to places you had closed off, but this process will allow you to become the integrated person you were meant to be. Let the parts of you that have been shut down and shut off have a voice, and learn to name what you needed in your painful moments—and what you need today. Trauma does not have to define you. In fact, when your moments of trauma are tended to and processed, they become your redemption story. The places that remained locked within your heart become the places where you find power and motivation to help others become free from their pain. Your calling begins to rise from the very places you felt bound but are now free. The Enemy doesn't want you to look back. He wants you to forget what happened and minimize the pain you feel, because he knows that once you begin to heal from your trauma and experience stirrings of freedom, you will want to expose him everywhere you see his scheming hand in the lives of those around you. Freedom awaits, friend, but you must acknowledge the places of trauma in your story so freedom can rise from them. And when your heart becomes free, you will partner with Jesus to help free others. Free people do, in fact, help free people.

Dear Lord, I long to be free of my negative self-talk. Please reveal to me the shame and the moments of trauma at the root of these thoughts. I don't just want to stop thinking these things; I want to uproot the reasons they began. I need your help. I know I can't do this on my own; I need you to help me and supernaturally heal me. I pray this in Jesus's name, amen.

CHAPTER 12

A NEW PATH

How many times have you heard the phrases "We're a fallen people" or "We live in a fallen world?" Fallen world? Yes. Fallen people? Well, kinda—but that's not the final word on who we are. We are a *resurrected* people. When we invite Jesus into our hearts, we're promised eternity with him in heaven. But what about while we're still on earth? Are we left to fend for ourselves, counting the days until God calls us home? Absolutely not. Philippians 2:12 (NLT) calls us to "show the results of your salvation," which I have come to understand means to experience heaven on earth—or, to live fully alive. Though we can't avoid the effects of sin while on earth, we can do our best to fight those effects by stepping into our traumas and inviting God to move us away from shame and onto a new path toward healing, wholeness, and hope.

This new path emerges once we do the work of identifying our traumas. Once our traumas are identified, we can engage them, identify what we needed and never received, and invite God to meet those needs so we can receive healing. Simply, it

means acknowledging that we've lost something or someone, and possibly also that we've never told anyone about it and therefore never received the care, comfort, or validation we needed at the time. It also means appropriately grieving the loss and actively sharing our story with others so we can move toward healing.

Let's start with the first part—grieving. Nearly all traumas involve loss, and losses require grief. Grief is not something we have been taught to do well. In fact, many of us have experienced shame around grief. We might experience shame, for example, if a loss occurs and we feel deeply about it, but instead of our emotions being met by kindness or tenderness from others, we experience contempt or dismissiveness. Contempt may sound like "Boys don't cry" or "Crying is for the weak." Dismissiveness, on the other hand, sounds like "God's got it" or "It's all going to work out." These dismissive statements minimize our grief and attempt to remove our emotions from the loss. But the emotions of loss have to go somewhere; if we don't tend to them, they will become lodged within us and create a sense of contempt or cynicism, which causes dismissiveness to form in our hearts.

If we want to live whole, we must lament our places of wounding, the parts of our story where shalom has been shattered. Does this thought intimidate or scare you? You are not alone. I commonly hear thoughts like "I don't want to stay in my grief forever" or "The sadness will overwhelm me and trigger destructive behaviors." These are legitimate fears, because if we don't properly care for our grief, we will become enslaved to it and move into despair. Thankfully, God has given us a crucial tool to equip us to grieve well: his Word. Besides the entire book of the Bible dedicated to lamenting (Lamentations), Scripture is littered with reminders that God is near us when we are grieving, when our hearts are broken, and when we are hurt. I can't state this enough: keep your Bible near you as you begin the process of grieving. The words of Scripture can allow hope to rise amid pain and remind us to invite the Holy Spirit to bring comfort and, in turn, healing.

Do you remember the cycle of false freedom we talked about in part 2?

Correctly grieving the pain and trauma in our stories builds a bridge over the valley of behavior modification—the place where we stay stuck in our cycles of false freedom—and allows us to move toward a life that is free and fully alive. When we connect with ourselves by acknowledging our trauma and then take our grief to God and others in lament, we find the pathway to true freedom: connection.

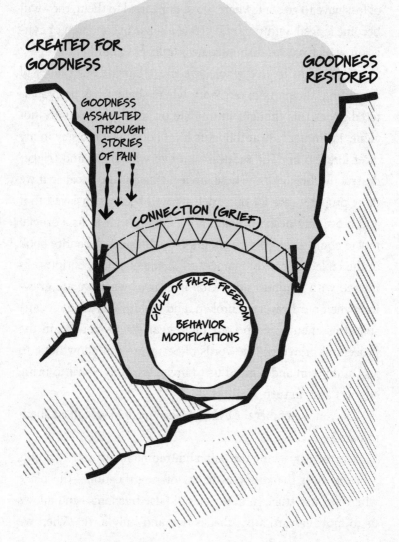

The Bible offers promises to guard our hearts, minds, and spirits on this journey. Avoiding pain is not one of them. To get to the victorious "I will fear no evil" part of Psalm 23 (verse 4), we have to go through the "darkest valley" part. But the beauty in that line sits in the word *through*—that means there's another side of the valley! This is a promise that we *will* be comforted, we *will* get through the pain of grieving, if we only choose to keep walking. God also promises us that we don't need to fear when we journey through our valleys, because he will comfort, guide, and protect us. Friend, this is so powerful! Remember when someone used to hold your hand when you crossed a busy street? Didn't you feel safe, even though you may have been afraid? Just as you weren't alone then, you are not alone when you grieve. God promises to be with you. He takes the posture of a good shepherd. He brings his rod and his staff to protect, comfort, and guide you.

Let's take a quick pause here for a Sunday school lesson— sans the felt board. A shepherd, as illustrated in Psalm 23, would use his rod to fight off danger and his staff to make sure the sheep stayed near him and didn't veer off the path. This is a picture of what God is offering to you. When you encounter painful places, God uses his rod to fight off the Enemy and keep him from taking you down, while his staff keeps you moving on the path toward healing. Your only job is to listen for the shepherd's voice and trust his staff as you walk. Easier said than done, I know—but the sheep learn to trust in the shepherd the more they surrender to his voice.

You will encounter pushback on your journey through grief into hope and healing. The Enemy wants you to stay stuck in the old path of trauma, the one that leads to shame and hate.

He likes it when your moments of hope are shattered by your own hatred. He is sinister in how he plays with your mind. The only way to stand in authority over him is to allow your soul and spirit to be tended to by the shepherd—and then engage in a head-on face-off against the lies the Enemy has spoken over you for years. This journey is not for the faint of heart, but Jesus says to you, "If I am for you, who can be against you?" (Romans 8:31, paraphrased). He will guide you every step of the way; he promises that "the truth will set you free" (John 8:32).

Aside from the need to grieve, you may have additional needs that were never met and have caused scars. This is especially true if you have never shared your trauma with anyone.

When we share our stories with a trusted friend and are invited to include all the shame-filled parts, we allow our shame to be engaged in a way it hasn't been before. Shame is a result of untended-to trauma; when someone responds to our shame with love and grace, we can move past the shame to discover where it came from. Trauma stored in our bodies then gets dislodged when we receive care and comfort and validation. The problem is that shame blocks us from identifying the real root stories that have caused trauma in our life. So if we want to dislodge trauma, it's not enough just to engage our shame; we must engage it with the intent of getting to the root. This is how we heal.

Sharing with others is a crucial step in the process of connection that leads to freedom: once we connect with ourselves by acknowledging our trauma and then grieve that pain and loss through connection with the Lord, we must then connect with others so that we can move past shame and secrecy.

Jesus offered us a profound example of healing through connection when he traveled through Samaria (John 4). He met a

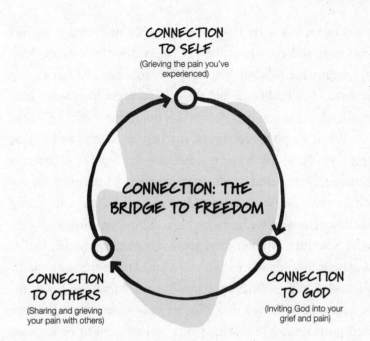

CONNECTION
TO SELF
(Grieving the pain you've
experienced)

CONNECTION: THE
BRIDGE TO FREEDOM

CONNECTION
TO OTHERS
(Sharing and grieving
your pain with others)

CONNECTION
TO GOD
(Inviting God into your
grief and pain)

Samaritan woman, who is now often referred to as "the woman at the well." This woman told Jesus she was just getting water, but she was clearly hiding from people—getting water in the middle of the day by herself indicated she was not part of the "in" crowd. When Jesus, a Jewish man, began to speak to her, a Samaritan woman, she was shocked. This went against all their societal norms. He sparked up a conversation with her, beginning by asking for water (verses 7–15). During the conversation, he told her about a source of *living* water, which she could drink and thirst no more. The metaphor was somewhat lost on her, but she was so down to not have to go to the well anymore (verse 15). Rather than telling her more about the living water, though, Jesus next told the woman, "Go, call your husband and come back" (verse 16). At that moment, she was busted, and she told a partial truth, stating, "I have no husband." When I read this passage,

I am taken aback by Jesus's response. In my mind it sounds cutthroat and even humiliating! He said to the woman, "You are right when you say you have no husband. The fact is, you have had five husbands, and the man you now have is not your husband. What you have just said is quite true" (verses 17–18).

When I read these verses, my first instinct is to feel that Jesus was being harsh and condemning, but I only feel that way because a harsh and condemning voice is so prevalent in my own mind. If we don't fully understand who Jesus is, including his character and his heart for his children, we can mistakenly read Scripture through the lens of our own misguided beliefs and harmful experiences. But when I read more about who Jesus says he is in Scripture, I see that Jesus is kind, and his forthrightness came from a desire to heal this woman, not condemn her. Jesus knows that shame and trauma need to be engaged and cared for before healing can occur. Jesus was not content to have this woman think he was just a good man; he wanted her to know he was her Savior and his love could cover her most scarred and shame-filled places.

For this woman to experience healing, she had to come face-to-face with and engage her shame. Shame can't live in the presence of empathy. As Jesus engaged the woman's shame by naming what he knew to be true, he didn't humiliate her or cause additional shame. His gaze of love and care never left her. He offered kindness where others had offered humiliation. He stayed present with her when others had left. He spoke kindly when others had spoken harshly. This time, when the woman came face-to-face with her shame, she did not feel humiliation as she had so many times before. This time, her shame was met with grace and mercy and love. Jesus knew that in order for her heart to heal, her shame had to be exposed so she could see there was a new way she could live.

After offering empathy, Jesus was able to move past the woman's shame and get to the root of her pain. This woman had experienced deep trauma. She had been betrayed by men, mocked by her village, and left alone, without the love she so desperately desired. But in this moment with Jesus, she was met with what she had always longed for: to be seen with all she had done but still be loved. To be held in all she had endured and be offered kindness. Everyone else saw her for her failings, but Jesus saw her as worthy, and he went out of his way to talk to her. It was a great risk for a Jewish man to speak to a Samaritan woman, but Jesus didn't care. The restoration and transformation of her heart mattered more to him than any man-made rule. Despite all that her story held, she was loved, embraced, and cherished. A woman who'd had six partners had probably been longing for these feelings her whole life.

How do we know that engaging the woman's shame got to the root of the issue and resulted in freedom? Because her actions tell us the story: *she ran!* As fast as she could, even leaving her water jug behind, she returned to the same villagers who spoke about her behind her back and wouldn't let her be part of the community's daily water-gathering ritual. She ran back to those same people and declared with joy, "Come, see a man who told me everything I ever did. Could this be the Messiah?" (verse 29).

Something happens when our shame is exposed and, rather than being condemned, we are held, cared for, and cherished. When shame hides within us, it breeds contempt for ourselves and the world around us. Cynicism and isolation become our places of protection, but they keep us from the love and connection we truly want. Jesus knows this. And it's not enough for us to *know* we are loved. We need to *feel* that love in our most unlovely places—the places where our stories of brokenness have been woven into narratives telling us we are unworthy and unloved. When Jesus engaged the woman at the well with the stories of shame she was bound to, he offered her freedom, telling her, "I see all you have done, and I love you anyway." Engaging shame is the way a story that has been stuck begins to shift. Confessing our shame brings restored intimacy with a God who loves us no matter what, and when we are loved despite our sin and mistakes, we experience healing and hope. We then see that our shame is the result of trauma that was not cared for, and we now have the opportunity to get to the root of why the shame is there in the first place!

You may think that by avoiding engagement with your places of shame and trauma, you are avoiding pain, but this isn't the case. You have just learned to numb the pain of heartache and settled for mediocre living—but God wants to step in and breathe new life into your story. He did it for the Samaritan woman, he did it for me, and he'll do it for you.

Dear Lord, help me to see that your redemption is not just for everyone else; it's for me too. You will meet my shame-filled places with love and care when I bring them into your light. I want freedom from the stories that keep me bound, and I will take courage that you are calling me right now to bring those wounded places before you. I am expectant that if you would go out of your way, break rules, and reveal yourself to someone the world would consider a nobody, surely you will do the same for me. Thank you for your Word, which speaks to me through the stories of other broken people met by a Savior who rescues. In Jesus's name I pray, amen.

CHAPTER 13

ACKNOWLEDGING OUR NEEDS

I've been married to my husband, Mario, for almost nineteen years, and in those years, I have had to learn how to fight well. The absence of fighting is an unrealistic expectation for relationships. Whether you fight with yelling or with stonewalling, you will inevitably fight. Because of this, marriage can be a battleground. And the battles I've fought with my husband are unlike any I've had or will have with any other person. Learning to fight well and fair has been a journey, and it's one I'm still on. Pray for my husband, please.

One night, a simple disagreement over the dishes escalated into a full-blown argument, and before we knew it, we were in the red zone. As the argument escalated, Mario finally yelled out, "What do you *need* right now?" It's rare for Mario to yell, so this got my attention. And his question stopped me dead in my tracks—not because the question itself was so profound, but rather because my immediate response stunned me: *care.* I needed care. I realized that while my head was saying, "Win the war over the dishes!" my heart was saying, "I feel fragile, and I need care."

This incident happened during a season of deep pain in my life. I was facing hurts from my past, financial struggles in my business, and an honest look at how I saw myself. I was a wreck internally. I was learning how to let God tend to my heart but wasn't holding space for the fragility I was experiencing. So, when Mario and I started fighting about the dishes, all my frustration and my past, present, and future pain came rushing to the surface. Old survival techniques kicked in, and I was going to manhandle my way to peace.

If a fight seems irrational, and the emotions involved seem disproportionate to the situation, chances are there are deeper issues at play. In my case, "The Great Dish Debacle of 2019" was not the real issue. When Mario asked his question, it was as if a great release took place. I was being given permission to share a need—to be seen and to *name* what I was needing. It felt like an offering of goodness and grace amid my turmoil. I was drowning in my emotions, and he offered me a life preserver. He didn't realize the power of his words in the moment, but I did. By asking what I needed, he helped me identify the emotion underneath my anger (grief) and then attach a need to that emotion (being held).

We are living, breathing creatures with endless needs and desires and longings. We aren't robots that plug and play, with systems in place to ensure that life can be "good." Humans are complex beings, because we were made in the image of a complex God. When Jesus lived on earth, he experienced a wide range of emotions. He felt compassion in his spirit when he encountered lost souls (Matthew 9:36), he mourned when he found out John the Baptist was killed (Matthew 14:13), he agonized over the sacrifice he was going to have to make on the cross (Matthew 26:36–46), and he was fatigued and needed to sleep when he was on the boat with his disciples (Mark 4:38). All these emotions show his humanity. And he didn't run from the emotions; he allowed them to have their place so the need attached to the emotion could be identified and met.

To respond to our emotions in a healthy way, it's not enough to just acknowledge them—we must understand the need attached to each emotion. Something happens within our psyche when we name what we need: our emotions connect to an outlet that moves us toward healing. When we don't attach needs to our emotions, they circle in chaos with nowhere to go. We are wired to bring resolution, to have a course of action. When we don't, we risk letting our emotions run rampant, which could lead to complete shutdown or a huge blowup.

The first step to recognize a need is to identify our emotions (revisit chapter 10 if you need a refresher on emotional language). Psalm 40:1–2 (NLT) shows us a beautiful example of recognizing an emotion and presenting that emotion before the Lord: "I waited patiently for the LORD to help me, and he turned to me and heard my cry. He lifted me out of the pit of despair, out of the mud and the mire. He set my feet on solid ground and steadied me as I walked along." These verses include a few indicators as to where the psalmist is emotionally and what he is doing with his emotions and pain. He begins by saying, "I waited patiently." Patience, also known as long-suffering, is one of the fruits of the Spirit. It seems almost sweet when we say the word, but in this context, patience is anything but sweet. It's arduous, it's long, and it involves deep suffering. The psalmist is able to acknowledge what he's feeling, which is despair. And, if you look closely, you can see what he did with that despair—he cried out to the Lord, acknowledging his need to be rescued.

What keeps you from naming your needs? Perhaps they were minimized or ignored in the home where you grew up. Or maybe you were required to meet the needs of a parent or sibling and received little care yourself. Whatever the reason, most of us have a hard time naming our needs. We struggle to put them into words, not wanting to seem too "needy," or we have become so cynical that we are convinced our needs will never be met the way we want—so why even bother to name them? These thought processes stem from a wounded heart that desires desperately for its needs to be met. Maybe it feels risky to ask for what you need. You have been let down so many times that it's easier to just do for others and become cynical or apathetic about your needs. The truth is that we are all in need; we are a needy people. This is not weakness; this is how we are wired. Remember, we are made in the image of God—a God who has never been alone and who wired us to need him and others as we journey toward healing.

You may be thinking that while this all sounds good, identifying the need behind an emotion can be overwhelmingly difficult. I've been there. When we are accustomed to self-reliance and survival, we shut down the parts of us that feel longing. So, it will take a bit of work to identify our deep needs. If you need help getting started, try doing an internet search for lists of relational needs—there are lots of lists out there that can help give you language to pinpoint and describe your deepest emotional needs. When you find a list that feels helpful to you, bookmark it so you can reference it whenever you need to.

Whenever you're experiencing an emotion, use the list to identify your need in that moment and offer that need to God or a trusted loved one. Notice that these lists are not about "fixing" your problems; they're about tending to the emotions you experience as a result. I can't promise that your problems will work out the way you hope. What I can promise is that when you name your emotional needs before God, he will offer his presence and care. On this side of heaven, his presence in the midst of heartache is the salve we need for our wounds.

We must trust God's timing. I think we often want immediate answers when we cry out to God with our needs. When we don't receive answers right away, we think the logical explanation is that the system (prayer) must be flawed, or we are flawed, or God is flawed. But the fruits of the Spirit are the outcomes of a mature life. God gives us these gifts, but they don't grow overnight. Just as a tree takes time to mature and grow and bear good fruit, so do we. It's in waiting (long-suffering) that we develop patience and learn to depend on the Holy Spirit. Our good God wants to break down our self-reliance and old ways of surviving so we will fully depend on him. Jesus came for two reasons—for our freedom and for intimacy with us—and we should always try to view his actions through the lens of this truth. He promises to be with you and to comfort your heart when you are in need, and he cannot break his promise. He knows best what will ultimately bring about your freedom. So we must trust God even when our trust in others has been broken. He *is* trustworthy, and when we continue to cry out and ask for what we need, he *will* answer.

You may be wondering, "What if I realize I'm angry at God?" All I can say to this question is that there are numerous

Scriptures in which God's children express anger toward him, and he is never intimidated or overwhelmed. I believe God is so gracious and so unbelievably loving that he will take your anger and help you find what's underneath. He'll join you in questioning your anger with kindness and curiosity, asking if there might be fear, unmet expectations, fatigue, or loneliness under all that anger toward him. When we offer our true feelings and needs to him, God helps us examine our thoughts and feelings so we can see their roots. This brings us closer to experiencing our true places of grief, connecting with our deepest selves, and in turn the grief brings us closer to comfort. So, don't run from God because you are angry, even if your anger is directed toward him. He can take it—and you need him to walk with you through it.

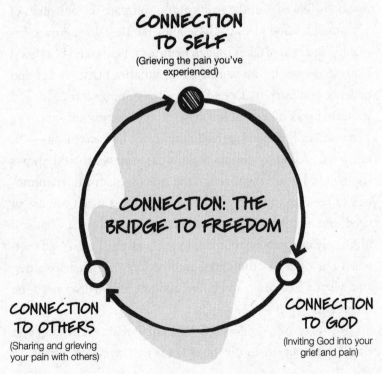

CONNECTION TO SELF
(Grieving the pain you've experienced)

CONNECTION: THE BRIDGE TO FREEDOM

CONNECTION TO OTHERS
(Sharing and grieving your pain with others)

CONNECTION TO GOD
(Inviting God into your grief and pain)

Matthew 11:28–29 tells us, "Come to me, all you who are weary and burdened, and I will give you rest. Take my yoke upon you and learn from me, for I am gentle and humble in heart, and you will find rest for your souls." These verses show us our need to learn from and find rest in Jesus. When we come to him, we can not only rest but also learn. This implies a relationship, a partnership, and a trusted connection. We don't "do business" with God—we don't just trade goods and services and move on with life. We are the weaker vessels in need of his tender and guiding care. Somewhere along the way, many of us have believed the lie that we are supposed to be tough, strong, and able to withstand whatever comes our way. Or we believe that having big faith means we shouldn't need much from God. But the reality is we are in desperate need of him every day.

Opening yourself up to identify your needs may feel risky. It leaves you open and vulnerable and exposes your heart, bringing the potential of being harmed or let down once again. But if you want to be free and fully alive, naming your needs is essential to your growth and healing. Jesus needed the Father constantly. He named his desires, his fears, and his needs before God— and received power to withstand rejection, pain, and even the process of death. When you let yourself name your needs before God and a few trusted people, you move closer to healing, and your heart can be tended to.

People will let you down; they can never fully meet your needs. We will always have needs, and those needs will never be fully satisfied until we reach heaven and our bodies are restored. But the good news is that Jesus promises to meet us in our needs. He promises to comfort us when our needs can't be met by others. He assures us he is not a priest who sits on high, unable to empathize with our weaknesses (Hebrews 4:15).

Naming your needs before God and others will keep you soft and tender. It will keep you close to the brokenhearted, close to Jesus, and far from the self-reliance that leads to pride and bitterness. Naming your needs is a pathway to receiving grace and mercy, which is then a catalyst to breaking the chains of self-reliance and loneliness. There is power in naming our needs before God, and it's only through taking that risk that our souls will find peace.

> Dear Lord, I am in need. I'm learning what it means to bring my emotions to you but am realizing I have permission to express my needs as well. Help me to come to you honestly with my emotions, and I also ask that you meet me in my needs. I will wait patiently, even if it means my suffering continues, because I trust that you are doing a good work within me—to strengthen me and bring about healing. Help me to trust you more today. In Jesus's name, amen.

CHAPTER 14

ENGAGING THE BODY

For about ten years of my life, I was a fitness trainer. In the season before that, I had gone through a painful divorce that left me shattered. My body was a wreck, and my mind was undone by all it was enduring. My therapist said to me, "Karrie, you need an outlet for all this tension you're holding. You need to exercise to ease the anxiety." So, I hit the gym, and it became my refuge. It was where I could let out all my aggression; it brought release during a season that felt like it was sink or swim. I loved working out so much that I went back to school to become a trainer and started my own personal training business.

Thanks to kids and a career in ministry, I eventually left the world of fitness behind to pursue those other growing passions. I still walked occasionally and would do a Pilates class here and there, but consistent exercise wasn't part of my routine anymore. Then one day my friend Meghan invited me to a barre class she had been wanting to try for weeks.

What happened next was ungodly. It was sadistic. It was torture. It was rude. The class instructor made us grab a small circular band, step into this band, and bring the band up to where it fit snugly around our ankles. She then proceeded to hand us each a small rubber ball to place between our knees. We were then instructed to lie on our stomachs. Are you tracking? There I was, lying on my stomach, band around my ankles, ball between knees, and this woman had the audacity to bring me two dumbbells to put in each of my hands. *What in the actual heck are we doing here???*

At one point, with about thirty minutes left in the class, I looked over and saw Meghan lying on the floor, face to the ground. She looked dead, and I seriously wondered if she was. This was a fair question in that moment. So, I whispered to get her attention. She just looked at me, moving very little of her body, and whispered, "This is terrrrrrible!" This memory makes me laugh to this day, because she said these words with such a depth of sorrow that every part of me felt it too.

Now listen, I wouldn't wish that experience on anybody. Meghan and I barely made it out of the studio with our dignity intact that day, but the truth is that barre class triggered something in me: a call back to my body. We spend a lot of time working on our minds and our hearts. This is good work, but we shouldn't neglect our bodies. Our bodies hold the glory of God. Now, before I go any further, I'm *not* talking about weight loss or depriving your body in hurtful ways. I'm talking about taking care of your body and listening to your body.

The Holy Spirit indwells our bodies, yet the amount of abuse and neglect we inflict on those bodies is painful to think of. First Corinthians 6:19–20 tells us, "Do you not know that your bodies are temples of the Holy Spirit, who is in you, whom you have received from God? You are not your own; you were bought at a price. Therefore honor God with your bodies." You are the keeper of your body, which was made to move, smell, taste, see, and feel. To engage the senses is to engage the body. Church culture often emphasizes taking care of our minds—gaining knowledge to better see and know our Creator. I'm not saying that's a bad thing, but if it's the only thing we focus on, we miss out on engaging with the Holy Spirit in the fullness of his indwelling. Our minds are prone to operate in survival mode, but our bodies tell the real story. Our bodies carry trauma, seek pleasure, and hold desire. We begin to heal on a visceral level when our body, mind, and soul are all engaged. In Bessel van der Kolk's helpful book *The Body Keeps the Score,* he writes, "In order to change, people need to become aware of their sensations and the way that their bodies interact with the world around them. Physical self-awareness is the first step in releasing the tyranny of the past."[2] Many of us live disconnected from our bodies. We have no idea what our bodies feel, but God does—and more than that, he deeply cares.

In 1 Kings 19:4–8 (ESV), we read about a time when Elijah was running for his life. He had just found out that Queen Jezebel was threatening to have him killed. Elijah was scared and tired and at the end of himself emotionally:

> But he himself went a day's journey into the wilderness and came and sat down under a broom tree. And he asked that he might die, saying, "It is enough; now, O LORD, take away my life, for I am no better than my fathers." And he lay down and slept under a broom tree. And behold, an angel touched him and said to him, "Arise and eat." And he looked, and behold, there was at his head a cake baked on hot stones and a jar of

water. And he ate and drank and lay down again. And the angel of the LORD came again a second time and touched him and said, "Arise and eat, for the journey is too great for you." And he arose and ate and drank, and went in the strength of that food forty days and forty nights to Horeb, the mount of God.

I love reading this. God sent *cake!* Here's the thing. Elijah wanted to die. He was fed up, exhausted, scared, and ready to die. But God didn't respond with "Come on, Elijah, I'm God. I gave you the ability to call down fire from heaven. Get up and let's do this!" Instead, God tended to Elijah's body. He sent cake, friend, because cake is holy. There ya go, it's in the Bible! And not only did he send cake once, but twice—seconds are permissible! God allowed Elijah to rest, sent comfort in the form of an angel, and nourished his body with food.

Our bodies need to be tended to and cared for. We need rest, healthful and life-giving foods, and movement, among other things. When we fail to care for our bodies, I truly believe we are dishonoring the glory of God. Now, please don't read those as words of condemnation. Rather, take them as permission to tend to your body with goodness. Taking care of your body is holy work. Play is holy work. Eating good food is holy work. An ambling walk is holy work. Meditating on God's Word and taking deep breaths is holy work. (And to be clear, barre class is *the devil's work*, but if you find connection to your body and God there, who am I to judge?) Much of the work we have done in this book up to this point has been holy work, and yet I would be remiss if I didn't also help you see the value of engaging your body.

Research shows that a slow walk can flush cortisol (your stress chemical) out of your system, and a good meal or smelling an oil or fragrance raises levels of dopamine (your happy-thought chemical). Deep breathing is known to help lower blood pressure, help manage depression and anxiety, and bring your nervous system to a state of relaxation.[3]

Our nervous systems protect us when we are in danger and allow us to connect to other humans in a way that brings deep peace. Our bodies are amazing; they are one of God's most profoundly complex and beautiful creations. You are a walking, living, breathing miracle, and your body is so good at trying to protect you and keep you alive. But our bodies need care just as much as our minds and hearts do, because they hold the stories and the trauma of our lives.

Your body has carried you through so much; it has been strong. That alone is remarkable. You are remarkable. You have permission to love your body. For some of you, this won't be that hard. But for others, I know this may be asking a lot. You may feel like your body is against you, or your body may feel like a prison. God wants to release you from this place of burden. I believe one of the tactics the Enemy uses is to get us to ignore or hate our bodies—to think of caring for our bodies as a waste of time. Perhaps he has been waging war against your body for years. Think about how many of the lies you may hear in your mind are attacks against your body: "I'm ugly, fat, disgusting." And then there are the outward lies from other people, magazines, social media, and the culture at large. It can feel like an all-out assault!

It's time to take our bodies back, to honor the glory they hold, and to see them with gratitude. When you do the work of honoring your body as God's creation, you destroy any hold the Enemy has had over you in this area. This is not just a good idea, something fun to do, or another chapter for me to write. This is a battleground—and one in which you have authority because of the Holy Spirit who dwells within you!

Over the next few days, pay attention to how your body responds to the nourishment you give it. If you find yourself feeling anxious or worried or overwhelmed, choose to care for your body in that moment. What does it need? A walk? Rest? Cake and water? A moment to breathe? Honor your body by giving it what it needs, then watch as your anxiety begins to decrease and the chaos in your mind becomes quieter. We take our cues from Christ himself, who paused often to pray and rest and seek counsel and eat. The list goes on. What we never see is Jesus abusing his body, shaming it, or neglecting it. He honors his body.

It's time to take back your body—not just to bring it to a state of physical health but to honor all its workings. Your body deserves good care. It deserves to be listened to and offered space to reset and heal. Start small. Pause at some point in the day and take a few moments to breathe and take an inventory of how you are feeling. Where are you holding tension? Are you feeling disconnected from your body, and if so, why? Is your body needing rest or activity? Does it need food or soothing in some way? Getting curious about what your body is feeling and needing will give you insight into what emotions or situations may need to be engaged; for example, you may be experiencing certain feelings due to a situation you are wanting to avoid. Your body tells the truth. Your mind may try to explain away or override the sensations of your body, but if you stop and listen to your body, you can gain a clearer understanding of what is happening. You can also then ask more questions of yourself, paving the way into a deeper state of healing. If we are indeed made up of a body, mind, and spirit, then we must not engage only one or two parts of our being. To truly experience freedom, we must allow our full selves to have a seat at the table. All parts are valuable; all parts need to be engaged and cared for.

To engage the body, first pause and ask yourself, "What is consuming my mind? What am I feeling? What am I needing?" In this state of curiosity, you can invite the Lord to help you identify the best practices to engage your body. Take some time to bless your body. Bless your legs, which have walked you through life. Bless your chest, which houses your most vital organs. Bless your hands, which have wiped tears and held love. Bless your strong back, which carries the weight of so much but has not broken. Bless your beautiful face, which beholds the glory of God. Lay down any hatred you may have toward your body, and embrace your body as a good vessel that continues to let you know the places within your spirit that need care. Celebrate the tenacity your body has to keep going. "After all, no one ever hated their own body, but they feed and care for their body, just as Christ does the church—for we are members of his body" (Ephesians 5:29–30). God cares for the body and calls us to do the same.

> *Dear Lord, I praise you for my body. I haven't always seen it as good or treated it as such, but my desire is to bring honor to you with my body. I want to listen for the truths it's trying to show me. I pray you will help me treat your creation with reverence and kindness as I become more aware of my body's needs. I pray this in Jesus's name, amen.*

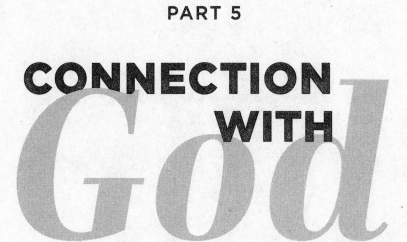

PART 5

CONNECTION WITH *God*

CHAPTER 15

GODLY GRIEF

As you pursue living fully alive and coming back to who you were created to be, connection with God is crucial. Once you've learned how to connect with yourself and identify your emotions and needs, you can invite God into those needs. This connection with God will help heal your wounds. This process is a lot easier said than done, though. It's painful and can be exhausting. It requires grieving—something we've often been taught to avoid or rush through. But when we invite God into the process, healing happens.

The world will tell you there are two ways to react to pain: "Be tough, bury your feelings, and move on!" or "Own your pain and make it your identity." But neither of these brings healing. It's unhealthy to let what has happened become your identity, but it's also unhealthy to ignore or bury it. Both options bring nothing but bondage. Allowing yourself to identify your pain and grief are central parts of healing. God wants you to acknowledge your heart before him.

Grieving what has been lost or taken from you is essential to moving forward. It is not weakness; it is strength. It takes bravery to face what has hurt you. Grieving your shattered expectations or the pain of your mistakes allows you to be cleansed from deep within and move forward. When you have unresolved bitterness and anger, darkness erodes your heart and freedom can't emerge. Take care when grieving your pain, though—many find comfort in staying stuck in this process. You may feel that because your grief is justified, you don't want to move on from it.

Grieving is a powerful part of the healing process, but only when we grieve with purpose. In the chart, inspired by Robert W. Kellemen's *God's Healing for Life's Losses*,[4] you can see typical responses to grief compared with healthy, biblical responses to grief. The biblical responses may not always take the place of the typical responses; in some cases they may accompany or follow them. For example, when we are wounded, our natural response is to be in denial or to isolate. Moving from the natural response to the biblical one, we see that we must get honest with ourselves about the feelings we are experiencing. This will be a powerful first step before we can move toward the next stage.

In 2 Corinthians 7:8–10 Paul is clear about the need for grief and its attachment to sorrow: "Even if I caused you sorrow by my letter, I do not regret it. Though I did regret it—I see that my letter hurt you, but only for a little while—yet now I am happy, not because you were made sorry, but because your sorrow led you to repentance. For you became sorrowful as God intended and so were not harmed in any way by us. Godly sorrow brings repentance that leads to salvation and leaves no regret, but worldly sorrow brings death." These verses show why grief is a crucial building block in the bridge over our cycles of false freedom. As we connect with God, he will bring to our attention

TYPICAL GRIEF RESPONSE

BIBLICAL GRIEF RESPONSE

DENIAL / ISOLATION

1

CANDOR:
Honesty with myself

Psalm 51:6 (ESV)
Psalm 25:16 (ESV)

ANGER / RESENTMENT

2

COMPLAINT:
Honesty with God

Psalm 6:3–6 (ESV)
Psalm 13:2 (ESV)

BARGAINING / WORKS

3

CRY:
Asking God for help

Hebrews 4:16 (NLT)
Psalm 40:1–2 (NLT)

DEPRESSION / ALIENATION

4

COMFORT:
Receiving God's help

Psalm 46:1 (ESV)
Isaiah 41:10 (NASB)

ACCEPTANCE / RESOLUTION
(typical response ends here)

5

CASTING:
Surrending the hurt

1 Peter 5:6–7 (NLT)
Psalm 55:22 (MSG)

6

CALLING:
Using your past pain to help others

Luke 8:39 (ESV)
Isaiah 61:3–7 (MSG)

Adapted and changed from Dr. Robert Kellemen's *God's Healing for Life's Losses*.

areas of pain that need to be grieved—whether pain we have brought on ourselves or pain others have caused us. There is deep sorrow in grief, but when we invite God into the process, there is comfort for us, and we won't move into despair. It's here that some of our most profound healing can occur. Lament cleanses our souls. It brings what has been in darkness into the light, and it breaks the weight of pain we have carried on our own.

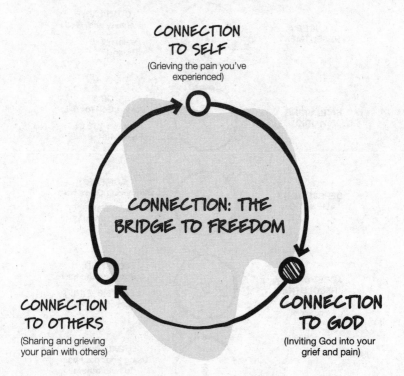

CONNECTION
TO SELF
(Grieving the pain you've experienced)

CONNECTION: THE
BRIDGE TO FREEDOM

CONNECTION
TO OTHERS
(Sharing and grieving your pain with others)

CONNECTION
TO GOD
(Inviting God into your grief and pain)

Grief will never end on this side of heaven. You will always be grieving something. Whether for small things or big things, grieving is part of the human experience. Grief is the great unifier, and when we honor and tend to our grief, we awaken deep compassion. We must stop running from the work grief wants to do within us. Grieving won't keep us stuck in our pain; in fact, honoring our grief allows us to move through the process of healing more honestly and allows comfort to come more readily. God meets our grieving with kindness, not putting a timeline on our pain but rather catching every tear that falls and holding it with love and grace.

Grief speaks to our longing—our knowing that it was not supposed to be this way. We were not supposed to die or feel pain or lose relationships. We were created for Eden, but we know that its doors have been closed and we must wait for heaven and its fullness to come. It's grief that keeps us honest and aware of our need for the presence of God every day. God uses our feelings of grief to help us identify the hurtful patterns in our story, the hold that people have had on us, the bitterness we may carry, or the pain we have had to endure. Our grief becomes an avenue in which our heart can begin to be cleansed as we express our hurt to the Lord. Processing our grief through connection to self, God, and others is the first step in a larger cycle that will lead us toward true freedom. When our grief and heartache are met with God's kindness, we gain hope that we can face another day—and we experience moments of heaven right here on earth.

> Dear Lord, what pain or loss do I need to allow myself to grieve? What stories need to be brought into the light so I can work through them with your comfort accompanying me? I believe that you desire for me to experience freedom by first naming what I have lost. In Jesus's name, amen.

CHAPTER 16

THE POWER OF INVITATION

Whۤen we're young, believing in God can feel simple and easy. For the most part, life is innocent, so believing isn't that difficult. Even those of us who grew up in trauma-filled homes may have still felt a sense of childlike wonder and carefree belief. In our young minds, God seems to be holding us in a way that feels unquestionable. We believe God is good and that's it. When we get older, our thoughts and feelings change. The world seems scarier, and the reality of darkness takes its toll. We see the world for what it is and have a hard time seeing the good, either in ourselves or in God. We fight to stay alive, or keep up, or just show up. Even our relationship with God, church, and faith is affected; striving for anything to help us feel free and fully alive becomes an exhausting game that we feel we can never win.

My next point may seem minor within the larger process of

acknowledging our emotions and naming our needs, but it is a truly important part of this journey to wholeness.

It's the idea of invitation.

God has given you the choice to choose him or not, just as my teenage son can choose whether to let me into whatever he's going through. This isn't just a onetime choice for salvation; it's a daily choice to invite God into every aspect of your life. Jesus won't force his way into your life. You are his child, but you're free to choose him or not. He will wait, he will call to you, but he will not force his way in. We have an active role to play; we must first invite his presence and then continue to seek him and his activity in our lives—we must continue to knock, to search, to invite. The door will always be open, and the searching will always lead to the presence of God. Whenever you invite God in, he will come. It's the beauty of the relationship you have with the King of creation:

> Ask and it will be given to you; seek and you will find; knock and the door will be opened to you. For everyone who asks receives; the one who seeks finds; and to the one who knocks, the door will be opened.
>
> **—Matthew 7:7–8**

Inviting God into our lives is part of our healing. We welcome him into our places of pain, secrecy, and isolation. Our invitation says to God, "In the midst of the feelings I'm carrying, I will offer my need to you." You may view God as a distant being looking down at you from the edge of the "pit" you have found yourself in; you may imagine him shaking his head with disappointment and yelling from the top, "What are you doing down there? Where is your faith?" Rather than invite God in, your initial response may be to feel shame and wonder, "How did I let myself get here? I better *try harder!*" You lean on your own strength as you try to crawl your way out. Internal thoughts swirl: "I know what I need to do—I need to work harder to get out of here. When I finally get it together, I can join God in all the good he is doing outside this pit." You might even make a bit of headway up the side of the muddy pit, only to be knocked down again by the heartbreak of life, the frustration of not seeing the results you want, or the isolation you feel from being stuck for so long. Your cry begins to change from one of shame and self-reliance to a desperate cry for help.

We often think that in order for God to help us, we must first do all the right "things" to help ourselves. We think we must say the right prayers, take Bible study courses, show up to church, and even volunteer—as if these actions will bring about the rescue we need. We use these behaviors as ineffective ladders in our attempt to climb out of our pit. These are all good things, but without the foundation of understanding our need for God's presence in and rescue from our circumstances, we will feed a cycle of false freedom, using behaviors to try to rescue ourselves from despair. Our best course of action is to issue an invitation to God, saying, "I am at the end of myself. I can no longer pretend that I can get out on my own." This is where Jesus can do his best work. Jesus *climbs down* and enters *into* the pit with you. I'm not encouraging a "just give it to God" mentality that keeps God far from you, but rather a true invitation for him to enter into your pain alongside you. This is relationship; this is where healing can begin. Jesus tends to your heart, he offers a salve for your open wounds, and he comforts you as you mourn (Matthew

5:4). When it's time, he picks you up and begins to carry you out. This process allows time for healing. Broken trust, hurt, and the self-reliance you cling to—God can wipe all these away when you admit you can't rescue yourself and instead acknowledge your need of him.

True relationships happen when we are honest and vulnerable—and when our honesty and vulnerability are met with kindness and care. We find deeper intimacy with God when we go to him admitting, "I've got nothing. I'm a wreck. I'm angry and sad and confused and alone. I need you."

The following psalm paints a beautiful picture of God joining us even in the dark places of our lives:

> Where can I go from your Spirit?
> Where can I flee from your presence?
> If I go up to the heavens, you are there;
> if I make my bed in the depths, you are there.
> If I rise on the wings of the dawn,
> if I settle on the far side of the sea,
> even there your hand will guide me,
> your right hand will hold me fast.
> If I say, "Surely the darkness will hide me
> and the light become night around me,"
> even the darkness will not be dark to you;
> the night will shine like the day,
> for darkness is as light to you.

> **—Psalm 139:7-12**

If you make your bed in the depths . . . *God is there*! Instead of Jesus peering into the darkness of the pit of despair to see you squirming on the ground, he wants to come down to you! When you are surrounded by darkness, he brings light. He can't bring light if he doesn't go *into* darkness. Something remarkable happens when you realize that this is what God's love is like—he wants to be with you even in your dark and needy places. You are free to need, free to feel, free to invite, and free to ask. Here's the deal: he will not bombard his way into your heart. The power comes when you ask. The power comes when you surrender your own attempts at healing and reach for his hand. You will have to choose to trust, even if just a little. You will have to get honest about how truly desperate you are in order for your heart to be ready for true healing. In response to your honest invitation, Jesus will bring his light to illuminate the darkness surrounding you.

Psalm 40:1–3 is one of my favorite passages in Scripture. It shows a clear picture of connection to self and to God, and it even speaks to how God will redeem our stories. In these verses we see the depths of pain David feels as well as his cry for help. Before God tended beautifully to David's heart, David had to cry out! David's honesty about the state of his life and his invitation for God to enter into his pit to rescue him created the intimacy needed for redemption:

> I waited patiently for the Lord;
>> he turned to me and heard my cry.
> He lifted me out of the slimy pit,
>> out of the mud and mire;
> he set my feet on a rock
>> and gave me a firm place to stand.

—Psalm 40:1–2

Inviting God into your life begins the process of repentance, which creates intimacy with God. This intimacy is necessary for healing and living fully alive. In previous chapters, I've shared the importance of connecting with yourself—identifying your trauma, feelings, and needs. Connection with God is the next step, and that's when the action begins. Invitation is action. *Knock* and the door will be opened; *seek* and you will find (Matthew 7:7–8). *Cry* out to the Lord (Psalm 34:6). *Come* to God when you're weary (Matthew 11:28). These action steps are on us. God pretty much handles the rest, but these actions are part of our role. They are all ways of inviting God's presence and activity into our lives. Identifying our emotions and naming our needs will only go so far in our ability to heal. We need supernatural intervention.

Dear Jesus, I invite you in—into my whole heart, into the stories I know I have been keeping from you, and into the stories that I have minimized. I invite you to comfort me but also to convict me of the sin that has so easily entangled me. I know you have more for my life, but I won't experience this without the filling of your Spirit and without your entering into every part of my being. Come, Holy Spirit, have your way and help me to walk on the path of everlasting hope. In Jesus's name, amen.

CHAPTER 17

WE NEED JESUS

Have you ever felt close to something you wanted, but no matter how hard you tried, it seemed to be just out of reach? The Bible tells a story about one man's desire to be healed and the lengths he would go to get well, and I'm struck by parallels I've experienced in my own life:

> Soon another Feast came around and Jesus was back in Jerusalem. Near the Sheep Gate in Jerusalem there was a pool, in Hebrew called *Bethesda*, with five alcoves. Hundreds of sick people—blind, crippled, paralyzed—were in these alcoves. One man had been an invalid there for thirty-eight years. When Jesus saw him stretched out by the pool and knew how long he had been there, he said, "Do you want to get well?"
>
> The sick man said, "Sir, when the water is stirred, I don't have anybody to put me in the pool. By the time I get there, somebody else is already in."
>
> Jesus said, "Get up, take your bedroll, start walking." The

man was healed on the spot. He picked up his bedroll and
walked off.

—**John 5:1–9 MSG**

The sick man in this story was so close to what he thought
would heal him but seemed to be missing the mark. He tried
for years to solve his problem. I mean, you have to give him
kudos for his tenacity. He put a lot of energy and effort into the
day-in, day-out ritual of trying to heal. But that pool was never
going to heal him. He needed the hand of Christ upon his life.
He needed intervention. He didn't need the pool, or the temple,
or the Jewish religion; he needed *Jesus*. I can relate to this story.
Although my body isn't broken on the outside, my spirit has
been battered and bruised, and I've tried many of the "healing
pools" the world offers in an attempt to solve my problems—but
none of them brought true healing. A similar story plays out
in many of our lives. The truth is we need Jesus. We need to
encounter him daily and continually seek closeness with him.
We can't experience healing without Jesus, and we can't stop at
our own actions; we need supernatural intervention.

Are there areas in your life where you have been trying hard
to find healing but feel like it's just out of reach? The Enemy will
present solutions that look like truth, smell like truth, and may
contain some partial truth, to keep you away from the actual
truth that will set you free. Many people settle for these solutions, thinking maybe that's the best they can get, and they never
experience the transformative love of Jesus. This Jesus knows
you intimately and wants to heal every wounded place in your
heart. We often opt for counterfeit paths to healing. We look to
self-help messages and natural remedies and even the desires of

our flesh to try to soothe the ache we feel, but I implore you to *want more*. The Bible says to seek and you *will* find, knock and the door *will* be opened (Matthew 7:7). In this verse and others like it, God is letting you know that nothing outside of him will fulfill the desires of your heart. The healing that feels out of reach is only possible through his supernatural power.

Don't live your life waiting for the offerings of this world to heal you. Seek true healing in the power of Jesus, who wants access to all of you for the purpose of restoring all of you. Without fully leaning into our need for Jesus, we will settle for counterfeit freedom and healing. Although these may satiate our sense of need for a while, they will always eventually fall short. Only when we turn our gaze toward Jesus, fall before him in honesty, and offer our story to him will we find the peace we long for. Surrendering to God will bring you back to who he created you to be, but you need Jesus as your mediator. Jesus says, "I am the way and the truth and the life. No one comes to the Father except through me" (John 14:6). None of our attempts at healing matter without Jesus. No connection with God is possible without Jesus. When we admit we need him, he responds. When we cry out to him for help, he rescues. When we desire to be made whole, he offers his presence. Jesus has always had his gaze upon you, but it's when you turn toward him, offer your heart, and invite him into your story that you will no longer desire counterfeit healing. You will know true hope has arrived.

> *Dear Lord, this prayer is simple. I need you. I lay down the idols that have kept me in a false reality. In my admission of needing you, I ask you to shine your light on me and reveal where I need you most. I pray this in Jesus's name, amen.*

PART 6

CONNECTION WITH

others

CHAPTER 18

WIRED FOR CONNECTION

I have had mood swings for years. And the lows within those swings have sometimes been *really* low. But I figured that I was an extrovert, so what goes up must come down . . . right? There were seasons when my mood dips would last for days or even months. I'd wake up in the morning and evaluate what kind of day I was going to have based on the weight of heaviness I felt in my chest. Most days I could power through, even when the weight made it feel hard to breathe. Those days I felt as if I were walking around in a fog. I was constantly on edge, and it felt like I had only two options for responding to my emotions: anger or tears. At first it felt easiest to just label these seasons as me being "overly emotional" and needing to "get it together." Maybe I just needed to pick myself up by my bootstraps, read my Bible more often, memorize more verses, or listen to some church services online. Do all those things, I thought, and I would be free from that heavy, low feeling. Did doing those things help? Not really, but I pretended it did, because I couldn't be bothered to spend the time to figure out what was really going on. And, if I'm honest, I didn't *want* anything to be wrong.

Then one day, I went to the doctor for a checkup. She gave me a test that indicated I had severe depression. First of all, this appointment was supposed to check my body to make sure it was working right as I got older—not to evaluate my mental state. Second of all, *what?* I mean, sure, I was sad a lot, but who isn't? Doesn't everyone wake up in the middle of the night—*every* night—and worry about all the things? Who doesn't need a good cry . . . at least once a day? As it turned out, these were signs of something deeper, something physical going on inside me that was manifesting itself in my mood. She asked if I had a professional with whom I could speak. I mean, yeah, I'd been going to therapy for years, but never did one of my therapists tell me they were concerned or that I had depression. In fact, I remember once asking my therapist if she thought I had a problem, and she just smiled and said, "No, you just have an extreme personality and need to learn to let Jesus bring you balance." I trusted her words, despite my own sense that feeling this down wasn't normal.

Though the news of my depression was a tough revelation, I chose to take it as something positive. At least I had a name for how I had been feeling for years, and now that the severity of the issue was glaring, addressing it became unavoidable. Around this same time, I decided to do some deep story work around my past and my present. Although the work was excruciatingly hard for me, something began to shift. I had fewer and fewer heavy days. The tears went away for days and then weeks and then months at a time. I was healing, and God was revealing the

truth of the darkness I had sat in for so long. Doing group therapy helped too; I felt as if I had a witness to my pain, and that
witness helped me feel tended to in the places that had felt so
broken. I thought, "Great! Bye-bye, depression, see you never!" I
now had tools in place, routines to maintain balance, and check-
ins with people for accountability. Everything was set up for me
to succeed.

Then, years later, the COVID-19 pandemic hit. Without my
realizing it, the constant pain, sadness, divisiveness, and trag-
edies going on in the world triggered a slow and steady decline
in my mental well-being. I watched my Christian brothers and
sisters at war with each other, and I saw fear and sickness rav-
age the world, all while trying to hold it together for the people
in my world and being stuck at home with no outlet in which
to experience community or care. The months went by, and
a familiar darkness grew in my heart. I tried to maintain my
mental-health practices, but they became just another thing that
I had to do. Isolation took its toll. Then, eight months into the
pandemic, boom, my whole family got COVID. Thankfully our
symptoms weren't too severe, but we still had to maintain strict
quarantine for twenty-one days. Things couldn't get any worse,
right? Wrong.

Literally right at the twenty-one-day mark, as we were getting ready to reenter the world, I woke up in the worst pain I
had been in since childbirth. I could barely stand or even lie flat.
Hours went by, and the pain became intolerable. We rushed to
the ER and found out I had a stomach ulcer. "Are you stressed?"
the doctor asked. "I mean, I'm fine," I said. We had been in full
isolation for almost a month and had recently moved to a new
state, I had just started a new job, and the weight of the world

was riding heavy on my shoulders. I was *not fine*. After a month of medicine, the pain went away, but the old familiar weight—which I had managed to live without for years—remained. I found myself crying in the shower, unable to deal with or put words to what was going on. But I told myself that the show must go on, so I trudged along.

One morning during this season, after a particularly long night of unrest, I went to a work meeting I'd had on my calendar for a while. Even though I felt overwhelmed inside, I knew how to push through—how to stuff whatever sadness I was feeling and come across well. While sitting in this meeting with two coworkers (who are also my friends), I got a phone call about a friend who was in the depths of despair. I immediately felt the weight of grief intensify, and I couldn't control my tears. I felt responsible for my friend and ashamed that my own medical needs had kept me from helping them sooner. I also felt myself relating deeply to what this broken friend was sharing. They were saying the exact words I was feeling. I couldn't hide my tears. Right there in that meeting, at that table with two coworkers who had only been friends with me for a hot second, I broke. I wept in a way that was totally out of the realm of what I thought was appropriate—sobbing, tears streaming, my face in my hands. I couldn't catch my breath.

I also felt a rush of shame. I was embarrassed and wondered how on earth I was going to recover from this. Accusations and lies spun rapid-fire in my head, as if someone was auctioning off every bad thing about me: "You're weak; you're stupid; they will never respect you again; how unprofessional; get it together; this is not how leaders lead." I sat there frozen in my chair, weeping. Now, I'm not afraid of a good cry. I mean, heck, panic attacks are something I'm quite familiar with, but crying like this in front of other people? Never!

Then something beautiful happened. As I wept, one of my friends looked at me and asked, "Karrie, are you crying for your hurting friend, or are you crying for you?" I sobbed even harder. He saw me. He could see past the surface explanation of someone else's pain and saw straight to mine. His wife, who was sitting across the table from me, followed up with "How long have you been carrying this weight?" Inside, I thought, "my whole life"— but this was the first time someone had invited me to let them hold my pain alongside me.

As I sat at that table, these two people who barely knew me held space for my heart and my hurt. They asked me questions and never, not once, tried to fix anything. They never prayed or quoted Scripture at me; they just tended to the brokenness I was holding inside. Despite how broken I felt, in this moment I also felt seen and beautiful. After I had shared what I was holding and feeling, one of my friends asked what I needed. She grabbed my hand, tears in her eyes, and let me know the two of them were not going anywhere. They were there for me. I paused. "What do I need?" I fought hard against the shame in my mind, against the lies that said, "You teach this stuff, you're a pastor, you should have it more together." I fought the survival instincts that were telling me to "get up and get out of there, don't show them any more of your heart or they will leave or mock you." I fought to tell the truth. I looked up and said, "Please don't stop being my friend after this." I felt young and small and weak. Vulnerability was a risky move for this fighter. My friend looked at me and said, "You have my word." Her husband took a breath and, with tears in his eyes, said, "I'm just so sorry you've had to carry this alone." They witnessed my pain and didn't run. They showed empathy to my heart rather than dismissing it. They held space for me, and it did something to me. When our time ended, I got in my car and drove away. I soon pulled the car over and began to cry again, but this cry was not a cry of despair—it was a cry of *relief*. The weight of grief had lifted, and the burden felt lighter. I had been seen in my weakness and was loved anyway. I had read Galatians 6:2—which tells us to "carry each other's burdens"—hundreds of times, but the truth is that I rarely let anyone carry mine.

In that moment when I was having a breakdown, I didn't need a Scripture or a prayer. I needed someone who was willing to sit in my pain with me and not be rattled by it. Do I need prayer? Yes, absolutely. Does Scripture give me life? You better believe it. But, in that moment, my heartache couldn't be bypassed with a prayer and a Scripture. It needed to be held. This was a kingdom moment. The Holy Spirit used these two coworker friends to tend to my heart. And he used them to heal the wounds I still held from when my heart had not been tended to as well. Jesus was using his children as a conduit for love and grace and care.

Community is God's design. At the beginning of creation, when all was good, there was one thing that was not good. God said, "It is not good for the man to be alone" (Genesis 2:18). God wasn't surprised by this. He didn't create the world and then get thrown off by an aspect of his creation. I believe this verse was put in Scripture specifically for us to read. God knew we'd tend to isolate ourselves. He knew how cruel this world would be and that the Enemy would often try to keep us isolated from relationships with people who care about us. He knew we needed to understand that isolation would thwart the full goodness we were created for. Sometimes I would love for my life to just be me and Jesus—doing life, hanging out, me growing under his teaching. These are all noble desires, but the problem is our stories often skew our thinking and, therefore, we need Jesus *and* a good community around us so we can learn from and be encouraged by others. A community of safe people can hold our hurts and help us follow Jesus with more honesty.

Thinking about the garden of Eden makes my imagination run wild. In my mind's eye, I see giant leaves, lush forests, and animals peacefully roaming around everywhere. I imagine the magic of Adam walking and talking and communing with God. They were naming animals together while Adam was learning and just being with God. Surely this was enough! I mean, perfect setting, hanging with God, living his best life! God even looked around and saw that everything was good, then proclaimed that this was so. That is, until he one day said, "It's not good." It's. Not. Good. Doesn't this strike you as interesting? I mean, the God of creation had been creating all the things and letting us know how good everything was. Why then tell us what wasn't good? Why not just keep creating good things and saying, "It's good"? It seems to me that God wanted to make something extremely clear, so clear that he chose only one time in his creation process to say, "It's not good."

God knew and wanted to make abundantly clear that something was off: Adam was alone.

But hold on, he wasn't alone. He had God. Surely that should have been enough for Adam! But God said differently. He said, "It's not good for man to be alone. I will make a suitable partner for him." It's interesting to recognize that God himself has never been alone. The Father has always been together with Jesus and the Holy Spirit. Let me write that again: God himself has never been alone! If God isn't alone, and he said it wasn't good for Adam to be alone, maybe it's not good for us to be alone either.

God made us in his image, and that image includes the togetherness that existed even before the creation of man. We are wired for connection. He knew we would need people who are like us, people who can help, and people who will walk with us and let us know we're not alone. Can Jesus sustain all our needs? Yes. Does this mean it's a good idea for us to isolate ourselves from others because we know this is true? No! God didn't design us to be alone, and he often chooses to meet our needs through the people and relationships he places in our lives. And God didn't just say aloneness was not good, but he also offered the solution to the problem: "I will provide a suitable partner for him."

The Hebrew word translated as "suitable" in this passage is *kenegdo,* and it has profound meaning. *Ke* means "like or similar." *Negd* comes from a Hebrew word that means "opposite or counterpart." God was essentially saying he was going to provide a companion who was like Adam but also different from him. The beauty of this is that God provided someone who was enough like Adam to relate to him, but different enough to bring a fuller picture of who God is to Adam. This is how the two were meant to support each other. Think about how often you choose to be with people who are like you. They may look like you, eat like you, listen to the same music, or have grown up in the same cultural background. Spending time with people who are similar to you may be comfortable and easy, but it won't show you the fullness of who God is or how we can glean wisdom from others to become more like Christ. In creating Eve, God offered a complement to Adam. Eve would complement Adam's strengths but also hold him in his weaknesses (the ones that were sure to come after the fall). God also designed them with similarities so they wouldn't feel alone in their humanity. The beauty of the garden is that it reminds us to embrace both the similarities and the differences between ourselves and others.

For us to truly walk in who God created us to be, we need to go back to the Genesis narrative and examine the moments of our creation. Genesis is our foundational story. It's where it all started. The way God created us in Eden was the way we were meant to be. Our bodies will always long for what was intended, as if we are foreigners trying to find our way back home. Eden beckons to us; we can sense that the fullness of who we were created to be lies in the story of our creation—and in community with others.

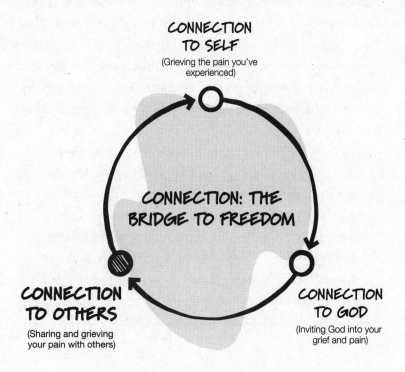

CONNECTION
TO SELF
(Grieving the pain you've
experienced)

CONNECTION: THE
BRIDGE TO FREEDOM

CONNECTION
TO OTHERS
(Sharing and grieving
your pain with others)

CONNECTION
TO GOD
(Inviting God into your
grief and pain)

God uses relationships to bring about parts of our healing. All the steps in the healing process are important. We need to acknowledge our own personal feelings and needs, and we need to invite God to tend and heal, but we also need each other. Many of our deepest places of pain have happened within the context of relationships, and therefore they need to be healed in relationship with others.

When I was crying at the table with my friends, God was inviting me into the next layer of my healing. I had done deep internal work, and I had walked with him through all of it, but now was the time for me to allow others to enter in. I had done this before, and a few times it was met well, but for the most part, I had suffered in silence. God took that option away in that moment; I believe he was showing me the goodness that can come when we allow ourselves to be held and seen. That goodness was part of his creation all the way back in Eden. My three areas of need were being met: connection to self through acknowledging my pain, connection with God by inviting him into the pain, and connection with others by allowing them to hold my pain.

> Dear Lord, open my heart to build meaningful relationships so that I can find healing. Help me identify those who are trustworthy and with whom I can share my story, so that we can together find healing and experience more of your kingdom here on earth. Teach me how to trust others and to be trustworthy when others share their story with me. In Jesus's name, amen.

CHAPTER 19

ENVY: THE GREAT DISCONNECTOR

I was in seventh grade when I first realized I was awkward. Before this awareness, I thought I was *all that*. I walked onto campus that year with such high hopes of being popular. I thought, "I'm *for sure* getting a boyfriend this year." That rite of passage had so far eluded me, but I thought junior high would be when all my dreams would come true. I was wearing a pair of Jordache jeans that were so tight I literally had to use a hanger to pull up the zipper, a Guess shirt, and LA Gear tennis shoes (for those of you who were born after 1970, let me help you understand . . . this outfit was a vibe and it made me a *big deal!*).

Sporting this fail-proof ensemble, I sauntered into my first-period class and sat down in the back, where the "cool kids" hung. Not a second later, the door opened and in walked what I can only describe as a junior high phenomenon—a unicorn by the name of Karley Cuaresma (yes, that was her exact name). As she opened the door, I swear I heard her own soundtrack start playing, and then the world moved in slow motion as she walked into the room. Her hair blew gently in a breeze that wasn't there as her perfect smile grew and lit up the room. My jaw dropped. She was stunning. And, in an instant, I became painfully aware that I was not. She was like Jessica Rabbit and I was like . . . SpongeBob SquarePants. Instantly, I felt shame. I still remember my thoughts: "I will never look like that. I can't compete with that."

Isn't it interesting and awful that my overwhelming shame in this moment—which took place twenty-some years ago—is still a memory I can relive vividly? The truth is that the Enemy catches wind of our feelings of inadequacy and he pounces. He takes one thought and plants it deep in our minds where it can feed more lies and deeper feelings of inadequacy. His tactic is to use those lies to isolate us. In the story of Karley Cuaresma and me, I soon began feeling envy and hatred toward her so I wouldn't have to feel the shame and embarrassment of not looking like her. I made up scenarios in my mind, assuming she was probably stupid or mean or whatever other terrible thing my preteen self could think up. Envy had taken root, and it caused hatred to rise within me.

Envy is ancient. It dates back almost to the beginning of creation. Not long after Adam and Eve disobeyed God and had to leave Eden, another relationship (so, another connection) was challenged—this time between Adam and Eve's sons, Cain and Abel. In Genesis 4:1–9, we see that they both brought an offering before the Lord. Abel's offering was accepted, but Cain's was not. Over the years, there has been much speculation about why one offering was accepted while the other wasn't (and, shameless plug, I once gave a message on it that you can probably still find on YouTube), but what I want to focus on now is how envy took root in Cain's heart. Genesis 4:6–7 says, "Then the LORD said to Cain, 'Why are you angry? Why is your face downcast? If you do what is right, will you not be accepted? But if you do not do what is right, sin is crouching at your door; it desires to have you, but you must rule over it.'" God was speaking to the state of Cain's heart, giving Cain an invitation to come to him and receive healing for his brokenness. God assured Cain that he would be accepted. God saw what was taking root inside Cain and offered a way out. But in the same breath as this invitation was also a warning. God told Cain that leaving his emotions unchecked would lead to destruction from the Enemy, who was waiting to pounce.

When envy consumes us, it's easy to lose control of our thoughts and become puppets whose strings are pulled by the Enemy himself. His goal is to keep us so consumed by envy that we disconnect from anyone who will speak goodness and life into our story. And if envy alone isn't bad enough, when it consumes us, we also fear that our inner thoughts will be exposed and we'll be rejected by others. In this way, the Enemy wages an all-out war on our ability and desire to connect with others.

The fear of being exposed can make friendships scary, especially when we've had experiences in which we revealed our true selves and it did not go well. We may decide we will avoid that kind of rejection at all costs. Why put ourselves in situations where we could potentially be hurt again? But as we discussed in the previous chapter, there's an answer to that question: "It's not good for man to be alone." Man, it can be difficult to believe that's true when we've been hurt by others. So again, we experience an inner battle between our desire to connect and our fears.

The reality is that no matter how much we fight connection with others, we will always long for it—because we were made for it. That yearning may be ignored or satiated by other things for a while, but it will rear its head time and time again. We can't escape how we were wired. Connection is such a strong need that researcher and author of *Lost Connections* Johann Hari has made videos and given presentations that demonstrate how a lack of connection with others drives addiction. His research proves that we are wired to connect; connection is how we thrive.

With this in mind, as well as the reality that connecting with others can be difficult when we carry wounds from past relationships, it's not surprising how often we become addicted to false senses of connection. Our brains will connect with anything we spend hours fixated on, from social media and pornography to streaming hours of TV. I see this crisis of disconnection in many people I encounter, but it's often masked by false senses of connection: "If I have a thousand friends on social media, then I'm connected." "If I'm using pornography to fulfill my unmet desires, then I'm connected." "If I can lose myself in a show or get fixated on global news, then I'm connected." None of these things can satiate the longing we have deep within us. They may numb us or create a false sense of connection for a while, but they leave us lacking true connection and addicted to whatever created the false connection.

To connect with others, we must get past our fear and envy and allow our hearts to be seen, tended to, and embraced. This can be scary when we have experienced deep hurt, but no matter how hard we try to avoid it, we can't escape our wiring. So, will you choose to press past fears, lies, and bondage to seek deep connection with others?

I didn't want to hate Karley, but my own insecurities led me to make assumptions about her to make myself feel more worthy. I felt less shame and pain when I made her the enemy. But what ended up happening was that envy took root in my heart and fed more shame. The rejection I was trying to avoid became exactly what I experienced—but it wasn't rejection by Karley or her friends; I was rejecting my own self. I took *me* out of the story. I rejected the idea that I had any goodness to offer the world, and this fed further isolation and rejection. Similarly, when Cain let envy take root in his heart, it turned into hatred toward his brother, Abel. This hatred was so intense that it drove him to kill Abel. The Cain and Abel story is a profoundly tragic example of how envy and the lies it tells us can lead to broken connection between God's children. Envy can begin its work in subtle, small ways, but if we don't bring our feelings before God, our envy will grow over time and breed disconnection, cynicism, and rejection.

It's worth noting that my Karley moment wasn't the only rough part of junior high. I spent a long time trying to fit in and find friends—I longed for connection! By the grace of God and the intentionality of some rare gems I met along the way, I did make a few good friends. How? Because they chose to seek me out even when I had all but written them off. They would stop me in the hallways to tell me I looked nice that day or that they liked my hair—silly things, but to an awkward junior higher who struggled with insecurities, these compliments meant the world. I am so grateful that these friends chose kindness and connection with me instead of envy, comparison, or jealousy. I have since realized God was teaching me and healing me through those friends, and for that I am so grateful. And I'm grateful to still be friends with a few of those girls, one being my dear friend . . . Karley Cuaresma! And yes, she still appears to have an invisible fan that blows her hair just the right way wherever she goes—but now I get to link arms with her and champion her glow!

Dear Lord, quiet any envy, jealousy, or comparison that is robbing me of deep relationships with people in my life. Teach me how to celebrate and champion others, bringing attention to how you are moving in their lives, rather than wishing their blessings were mine. Show me how to press past fears, lies, and bondage to step into connection with others. In Jesus's name, amen.

CHAPTER 20

HEALTHY CONNECTION

For many years, my understanding of connection was unrealistic and incorrect. I thought I needed an abundance of connections in order to heal. But large numbers of people overwhelm me. I want to have deep, meaningful conversations, and I can't do that with a long list of people. I would compare myself with girls who had a mile-long list of friends and think less of myself because I had maybe one or two. I hadn't yet learned the wisdom of pursuing "quality over quantity" in friendships. I also was under the impression that geography played an important role in meaningful connection—meaning I thought you had to live in the same place as your friends. This disqualified me because I moved so often—and have continued to do so into adulthood.

I also used to believe real connection required years of investment. I do still believe that growing deeper in our connections allows us to share more deeply what is in our hearts, but it's not necessarily years spent together that makes that happen. First Samuel 18:1 tells of the moment when Jonathan met David: "Jonathan became one in spirit with David, and he loved him as himself." Sometimes our hearts just know when we meet a kindred spirit. Time can help create close connection too, but often it begins with just a knowing—a connection that happens because the other person chooses to connect and see you rather than reject you.

The expectation that we must spend tons of time with someone to connect with them can be far too much pressure. It has been for me. In fact, I run at any sign of someone needing me too much, because the reality is that I have a lot going on; I am for sure going to let them down and fail to meet their expectations. Again, friendships for me are more about quality than quantity—including when it comes to time together.

Connection to others can happen in numerous ways. But I don't think the "how" of connection is the most important question; rather, it's the "who." What kind of people should we connect with? What kind of people must we be to create healthy connection? If connection with others is essential for our healing, then we need to know what type of person creates the right environment for healthy connection.

I think we can all agree we desire safety in relationships. Safety is the number one requirement for healthy connection. When we have been trampled on, mocked, abandoned, rejected, or betrayed in the past, we need a safe harbor that will protect us from such pain. Ecclesiastes 4:11–12 (MSG) paints a picture of the comfort and protection others can provide: "Two in a bed warm each other. Alone, you shiver all night. By yourself you're unprotected. With a friend you can face the worst. Can you round up a third? A three-stranded rope isn't easily snapped."

I love this version of this verse. I relate to the image of being alone at night, shivering—what a brutal feeling. I have felt God's presence in the darkest of nights; he has been my rock and my foundation. But some of my greatest healing, the kind of deep healing that leads to freedom from suffocating bondage, has happened when my pain was witnessed and tended to by human hands. God has used those moments to help me face the worst places of my story. He used his people to create the safe space where Jesus could ultimately heal my heart. Perhaps you have been hurt deeply by past relationships; you trusted, but it did not go well. But the Scripture is clear: "By yourself you're unprotected." Lack of protection leaves us vulnerable to the Enemy's attacks. It leaves us subject to lies that keep us stuck and playing small.

Neuroscientists have studied the physical effects of trauma and found that the hippocampus, a part of the brain, shrinks when it encounters trauma. This is a big deal, because the hippocampus helps with reasoning and regulates our fight-or-flight response. What does this have to do with connection to others? Well, when traumas are shared and grieved in a safe environment, the hippocampus begins to grow again, regulating thought processes and allowing us to think rationally instead of fearfully.[5]

This helps us work past our fear of trusting or engaging with others, because our brains can reason more easily. How cool is God? He literally wired our brains to heal in community! (By the way, I'm in no way a neuroscientist and my explanation is a drastic simplification of how the hippocampus works. If you're interested in learning more, I encourage you to look into Dr. Caroline Leaf's work. She *is* a neuroscientist and is amazing at explaining how our brains work.)

To foster healthy connection, we must create safe places where people can let down their guard, share honestly, and be held without judgment. We must listen and be curious about what it has been like for them to be them, and invite them to bring what has wreaked havoc in the darkness into the light. We must remember that we also were once in darkness and, in fact, may sometimes feel that darkness creeping in again and need safety ourselves. Offering light in dark places is truly a gift from God that will allow healing for the hardest of stories. As Ephesians 5:8 so beautifully tells us, "For you were once darkness, but now you are light in the Lord. Live as children of light." We have the opportunity to be the light of Christ, which will offer tremendous hope to those who share their stories with us.

Another key component of building healthy connections with others is having the wisdom to know whom to share with and how much to share. As fragile as you are, so is every other human out there. We are all trying to heal from our own hurts and past traumas, and we won't handle every situation perfectly. When we are thinking of sharing with others, we must first look at their character. I often observe people in group settings and am always careful to ensure that they honor each other's stories, are not quick to "fix," and don't gossip about others. It's healthy to exercise caution before sharing the fragile places of your story; wisdom helps you identify those who will be safe places to share.

Due to the high degree of care I take in identifying my safe places, I have experienced seasons when I had no one to share with. For whatever reason, God didn't have me in a place where I felt comfortable to share, or else I felt the people around me would not hold my stories with kindness. In those seasons, my therapist became essential. Therapy isn't free, so if you're interested in trying it but financing is a challenge, consider looking for ways to affordably make it a part of your support system, such as sliding scale payments, group therapy, or long-term payment plans. Your mental health, and having someone hold space for your heart, is essential to keeping the Enemy at a distance or at least identifying lies that are keeping you stuck. Not everyone is safe to share with, nor should you share with everyone. Safety within connection feels like someone saying, "I will carry the weight of your unfinished story with you." This sense of safety settles the heart and allows for more healing and growth to come.

Healthy connection is also built out of a heart posture that desires to serve and learn—and this can be hard to find. My friend Jamie is this kind of person. As soon as I met her, she offered to help me. She was willing to take my kids when needed; she came one day and cleaned my house (can I get an "amen"?); she stayed up late when I needed to talk; and even while she was serving me, she would want to know what God was doing in my life so she could use the knowledge I had to help grow in her own walk with Jesus. When I think of an apprentice of Jesus, I think of Jamie. For at least a year, I would first reject her offers to serve. Then she would insist, and I would acquiesce because, honestly, I needed the help. But I still thought, "Isn't it beneath her to serve me? Surely God has more for her than cleaning my toilets and taking my kids for a weekend?" These thoughts continued until, a few years into our friendship, I found myself offering to help another woman with her kids. As Jamie served me, I was learning to be more sacrificial with my time. This created opportunities to build connections with people I might otherwise have missed. The whole time Jamie was serving me and learning from me, God was using her to change me!

A humble posture of serving and learning takes safety to another level. I trusted Jamie with my heart because she modeled an aspect of Jesus's character that I lacked. It was through

Jamie that I began to see what Jesus meant when he said, "Whatever you did for one of the least of these brothers and sisters of mine, you did for me" (Matthew 25:40). In this passage Jesus is explaining that when we offer care and sacrifice, whether clothing someone or feeding them or offering care when they are sick, it's as if we are indirectly caring for Jesus himself. Jesus is essentially saying, "When you do these things for anyone, you are doing them for me."

Connecting with others allows us to share the heart of Jesus with a lost and broken world. And it's through connection that we also begin to heal. Burdens we've long carried become lighter as we step out of our stories and into the stories of others. As we serve and learn from one another, our unmet needs are met by the hands of God's kids. Allowing Jamie to serve me healed me. She provided nurture that I'd lacked as a child. I had longed for care but felt I had to "be strong" and not show any weakness. Connecting to others through serving and learning can heal wounds that run deep. And serving doesn't have to look like doing menial tasks; it's simply a heart posture that says, "I choose to put your needs over mine." When good boundaries are in place, serving can bring about immense healing—for both you and the people God brings into your life.

> *Dear Jesus, give me wisdom to identify the friends who are safe places to share the painful parts of my story, and teach me how to build healthy connections with them. Show me any boundaries that must be drawn to keep my relationships protected, and teach me how to serve and honor those with whom I build relationships. In Jesus's name, amen.*

CHAPTER 21

SAFE ACCOUNTABILITY

If you've attended church for any amount of time, you've probably been told that you needed to be in an "accountability group." In church circles, this phrase often means "a group of men or women to sit with and discuss all your struggles and, more importantly, how you're going to try not struggling with them next week." Maybe you're like me, and you've sat in these groups with fear because you know you're failing, and what good does it do to talk about it and add to the shame you already feel? Yes, accountability in relationships is crucial, but groups like this are not always the best way to achieve it. Accountability should feel like encouragement, not interrogation or a shame walk of all the things you did wrong over the past week.

Healthy connection with others does not involve condemnation or shame. Scripture shows us that God wants us to encourage one another. Hebrews 10:24–25 (ESV) says, "And let us consider how to stir up one another to love and good works, not neglecting to meet together, as is the habit of some, but encouraging one another, and all the more as you see the Day drawing near." This sounds like a far cry from meetings that leave us feeling beaten up because we couldn't "get it together." These verses describe an accountability that offers *encouragement* while maintaining connection.

To encourage someone means to give them support, confidence, and hope. When looking for healthy connection, we need to find people who are *for* us, who want God's best for us and will walk through the deep waters to help us understand *why* we are struggling with certain behaviors. This doesn't mean there's no place for warning or speaking hard truths, but if a person's goal is just to set us straight or fix us, they're not leading with a spirit of love. We must make encouragement an essential part of holding one another accountable. And to be clear, encouragement is not a passive "you do you, boo" kind of posture. Encouragement is bold. It's willing to name another's hurt and hold it. Encouragement speaks against oppression and offers truth. It's motivated by love and a humility that says, "I have been here too; you're not alone."

If we want to create a safe space where people can heal in community through the work of the Holy Spirit, we must create a space where words and actions of encouragement come first. Here are three key components of this kind of space:

1. Active Listening or Attunement

James 1:19 tells us, "My dear brothers and sisters, take note of this: Everyone should be quick to listen, slow to speak and slow to become angry." If we could master the behaviors described in this verse, we would create a deeply safe space for hurting people. When we are quick to try to "fix" someone or their problems, we bypass truly seeing the person because their pain or situation makes us uncomfortable. A mindset focused on fixing people keeps the people themselves at a distance and is the number one killer of connection. Instead, Scripture tells us to *listen*.

2. Empathy

Empathy is the ability to take on someone else's perspective and feel with them. It can be easy to try to fix others, especially when we see their brokenness leading them to sin. But meaningful connection won't happen if we jump into correction. If we instead empathize and listen while asking good, curious questions, we will create a space in which the Holy Spirit can illuminate the places in a person's life that need healing. Corrected behaviors will come in time, but it's not our role to force them. The Bible encourages us to have hearts that are willing to "carry each other's burdens" (Galatians 6:2). This does not mean that we are to take others' burdens and make them our own, but rather we are to carry the burdens *with* them as they hold the weightiness of life. The question is, do you trust Jesus to heal his kids' hearts? We must remember that we are not the Savior, and we don't have to rescue anyone. Most people are just looking for a safe space to be heard and known. These spaces are where God does his best work.

3. Comfort and Care

When we love from a place of care for our brother or sister, we allow their stuck stories to come out into the open, no longer bound inside creating pain and a sense of isolation. God uses his people to be his hands and feet. When we care for others well, we validate the pain they've felt, which in turn creates in them a greater trust that Jesus will heal their wounds. First Peter 4:8 tells us, "Above all, keep loving one another earnestly, since love covers a multitude of sins" (ESV). This partnership we experience with Jesus is holy and sacred and, when we enter into it with a heart of encouragement, can heal some of the greatest strongholds.

Safe, encouraging spaces allow people to confess their weaknesses without fear of judgment. James 5:16 encourages the practice of confession: "Therefore confess your sins to each other and pray for each other so that you may be healed. The prayer of a righteous person is powerful and effective." There is something profound about confessing to one another. It's mutual. It's intimate as you pray for each other, and it's empowering. Confession is not about shaming; it's about healing. It is crucial to choose wisely the people to whom you confess. Guard your heart and understand that your story is sacred. When you share it with someone, you're handing them a treasure, and whoever gets the honor of holding it needs to be worthy.

No matter how we look at it, connection with others is mandatory if we want to experience healing in our lives. Becoming who we were created to be will involve letting other people see us and know us. It's going to require us to get back out there, even though we have been hurt. Doing this work in our own lives will also enable us to help others along the journey. You don't need to be perfect to help others (that's an impossible expectation this side of heaven), but you do need to allow God to work within you so he can also do his work through you.

When I bawled in front of my coworkers and let them see my pain and join me in holding it, I knew I was in a safe space. We connected deeply because of it. So you can imagine how devastated I was when they moved away only months later. I had opened up and been vulnerable, which is so rare for me, and they held my story well, which is also rare . . . and then they left. When they did so, I had two options: either crawl back into my shell or else choose to see that their presence in my life, although brief, was good. It hurt when they left, but I'm a better person for knowing them. God used them to break down the stigma I felt around my mental-health issues. Instead of seeing me as the total sum of my brokenness and thinking my issues were too big, they met my pain with active listening, empathy, and care. They showed me that my issues were just wounds that needed love.

> *Dear Lord, thank you for always showing me the path to greater healing. I know that you desire peace for my heart, but so often it is hard to trust when I have been wounded. I know my heart needs care for it to continue to heal, so I will step out in faith and seek a trusted friend with whom I can share a bit of my story. You have designed us to rely on one another to keep each other moving toward a path of righteousness. Help me, Lord, to choose with discernment those I should share with and open up my heart to. Don't let me stay stuck in isolation and fear. I am worthy to be loved and to be cared for by you and others. In Jesus's name, amen.*

A CALL TO *home,* A CALL TO *you*

RELEASING THE OLD, STEPPING INTO THE NEW

During my process of getting honest about the stories from my past that held me hostage, I had to come to terms with the fact that many of these stories involved my family and my early childhood memories. It was hard to name the harm my parents had caused. Growing up Christian, I was taught that I must honor my parents; part of me felt that doing so meant never challenging them, exposing them, or being disloyal in any way. Naming the truth of what I experienced as a child caused major disruption in my heart and within my family. But not everything in my home was okay, and I had to name the truth of my negative experiences to heal. Not only did I have to name the truth, but I had to recognize how these experiences had affected my life.

I wrestled with Ephesians 6:2–3, which says, "Honor your

father and mother . . . so that it may go well with you and that you may enjoy long life on the earth." Wouldn't naming the harm dishonor the people who raised me? I wanted to defend them and explain why they did what they did. I wanted to preserve their reputations and deny any responsibility they had in causing me harm. I mean, they're only human, and they mostly did the best they could. Wasn't that enough?

To honor means to hold in high respect or great esteem. Naming what happened to me didn't mean I no longer could appreciate or even esteem my parents; I just needed to name the truth of my experience so I could be free. Avoiding the truth of my past, sweeping it under the rug, or lying about it would not have honored my parents. It would have set up our family for continued sin and allowed the Enemy to run rampant. Without telling my stories, I would have been setting up a future generation to live in the same bondage I, my parents, and even their parents before them had experienced.

My home wasn't terrible, but there were a lot of secrets and shame and brokenness, and much of the weight of this landed on me. I acted out for years, trying to make sense of the world I was living in. When it came time for me to share some of my stories, I saw the profound impact they'd had on me. I had to reevaluate what honor meant and run that definition through truth.

Don't mistake avoidance for honor. Honor comes from love and respect. If I truly loved my parents, I wouldn't lie to keep them from experiencing pain. By avoiding the truth, I was essentially keeping them from seeing areas of *their* lives that God may have wanted them to acknowledge. I was also keeping us from having a better relationship—one built on honesty and honor.

You may never come face-to-face with those who caused

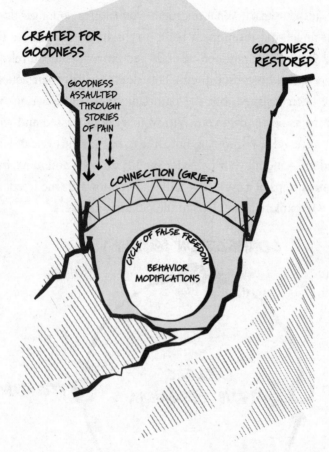

harm in your story. Even so, when you bring those stories into the light of day, sharing them with a trusted person and a good God, God will begin redeeming your story. If we don't face those childhood stories, we'll stay forever in a cycle of behavior modification—a cycle of false freedom. But when we name our places of harm, grieve their impact, and process the sorrow of how much they hurt, we can bypass those coping behaviors and move into heart transformation.

Over time, if you have grieved well, something begins to shift in your heart. What once held you captive no longer does. Your anger and resentment begin to dissipate. You release the hold your early childhood wounds had on you, and you release the people who caused them. This doesn't mean their actions have been justified, but the pain caused by those actions no longer has power over you. With your grief processed and your past hurts released, you are now free to bypass the cycle of false freedom—and all your behavior modifications—and move into the next steps of a cycle that will lead you toward true freedom. We will explore these steps in the next few chapters.

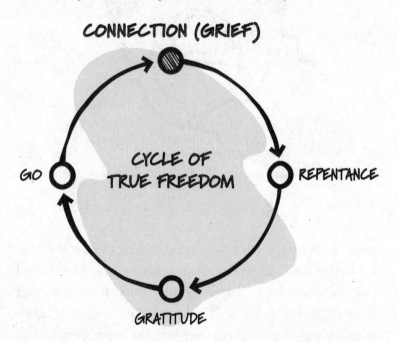

When I use the word *release,* I don't mean saying a one-time prayer and hoping everything will be good from then on. Releasing our past is a process, and one that we sometimes have to repeat daily. Release means looking to God and continually asking him to help you let go of your hurt. Releasing the pain and heartache of our past is not something we can do fully on our own. We need a renewing of our minds. No matter how many tools we have or steps we take, at the end of the day, we need a supernatural exchange to happen within our bodies and minds:

> Do not conform to the pattern of this world, but be transformed by the renewing of your mind. Then you will be able to test and approve what God's will is—his good, pleasing and perfect will.
>
> **—Romans 12:2**

This Scripture tells us that we must reject this world's way of thinking. The world is all too quick to say, "You're good enough on your own, what's past is past, and if you really want transformation you are going to have to do it yourself." The Enemy loves to whisper these lies of isolation and self-reliance. He knows that if you rely on your own abilities, you will never come close to the transformation God desires for you or experience the fullness of God's redemption in your story. The Enemy knows that even within the church we often attempt to heal ourselves through behaviors (Sunday worship, serving, Bible studies, forced quiet time) rather than through the true surrender of our whole selves. And even when we do surrender, we have a tendency to drift back into self-reliance and take back control of our lives from God. Speaking for myself, I know that I will often surrender and then take back, or let go of but then return to the same lies and hurts. I opt for behaviors that make me feel free momentarily, only to get stuck in a cycle once again. But when I invite Jesus into my journey and choose to trust him, he begins to renew my mind. Renewing the mind is an inside job—one that the Holy Spirit will do for you when you allow him access to all of you.

You will never be able to "think" yourself right. You will never be able to redeem your story on your own. You need supernatural intervention, along with a willingness to get honest with yourself, God, and others. Then your painful stories will no longer have power over you—you will have power over them. You will be able to see God's plan for you more clearly. You will be able to discern more clearly what is good and honorable and pleasing to God. The lens through which you once saw your life will change, because the stories of harm that kept you from God will be tended to. You will be able to let down the walls that kept you from the Father all these years.

Releasing your past also looks like forgiveness. Often in church settings, we're told to love Jesus and to forgive others— the end. I don't disagree that these two steps are essential, but as I have worked through my story, I've realized forgiveness flows from a heart that has been held and comforted in the midst of its own pain. I become more willing and able to forgive once others and God have witnessed my pain and named the truth of what they see. The beauty of empathy is it gives us a glimpse into the heart of God—a father who feels *with* us rather than from a distance.

Empathy means understanding and actually feeling what others are feeling. Experiencing empathy from others allows our own heart to be held and comforted, not fixed (that's God's job). It makes us feel that we've truly been seen. We become able to forgive, because our painful stories have been brought to the light and the truth has been told. When we experience love from God and others when we share, the pain of our stories no longer stays stuck in our bodies or our minds.

I became able to forgive more fully and release what I had been holding after I learned to have empathy for *my* story. I started with empathy for myself. Back to that popular saying at the Allender Center: "You can't take anyone further than you're willing to go yourself." My heart grieved for the little girl I once was, the one who felt scared and unseen. I wanted to weep on her behalf, for the years she thought she had to perform to prove herself to God and the world. I was able to grieve for what she needed and didn't get. While I was grieving, empathy rose within me; feelings of kindness and tenderness flooded in. This changed everything. The Enemy had been fooling me for so long, telling me that I was fully to blame for my broken life and that my needs were too big or invalid. Having empathy for myself allowed his voice to be silenced. What a gift God was giving me. On the journey to heal, I found who I was always meant to be.

This newfound empathy spilled over into all my relationships. I began releasing feelings of anger and resentment I'd held on to for too long. I was truly forgiving people I had once forgiven only in my head. My feeling of being stuck and confused began to lift. Knowing the pain of others' stories and realizing the pain of my own allowed me to see that despite the pain and shame, God was with me in the mess. Everyone in our lives has stories that have wounded them—our parents, our siblings, our spouses, our children. None of us may ever forget the painful experiences that have wounded us, and we shouldn't. To forget our pain would also mean forgetting the redemption Jesus has accomplished within our stories.

Jesus himself still carries his wounds, even though they've been redeemed. His resurrected body still carries the scars from the nails that pierced his hands and feet (Luke 24:40). He carries the story of what he did, the pain he suffered, and the power of that moment for all eternity. He didn't experience the shame of the cross and the heartache of being separated from his Father and then forget it all. He carries those scars so we will never forget what he has done for us.

Jesus is able to forgive *and* forget our wrongdoings, but even though we can choose to forgive, we cannot force ourselves to forget. And God does not expect us to forget our pain as part of our healing. We will remember our pain, but the work God does in our hearts will free us from the bondage that pain has had over us. To release is to forgive, and forgiveness is essential to healing, but we can't just jump straight to forgiveness and bypass the necessary work of uncovering and tending to the stories that need to be named, witnessed, and grieved.

The whole point of the gospel is that Jesus died for us *while* we were still sinners (Romans 5:8). And he is not a high priest who cannot empathize with our weaknesses (Hebrews 4:14–16). He experienced pain and grief and woundedness, and he always knows what we are going through. The gospel of rescue is ongoing. It's a daily journey involving our need and the revelation of his love for us. Every day, we can let the Holy Spirit lead us to the places in our hearts that need healing. Slowly but surely you will learn to forgive both yourself and others, and this freedom will help you to release anything still binding you to your past.

Dear Lord, I know forgiveness is essential to my healing. Help me, God, to honor the process of what must be done to truly forgive. Help me grieve my losses and not bypass the woundedness of my heart. Give me the courage to let you into the process so I can release the hurt I carry. Help me to honor the stories of hurt I carry by grieving, and through this process would you move me to deeper places of forgiveness? I pray that when I offer my heart to you, you will make a supernatural exchange and set me free from what has kept me bound. In Jesus's name, amen.

CHAPTER 23

REPENTANCE

Do you have a favorite word in the Bible? Maybe it's *love* or *grace*, or maybe it's *mercy*? It's probably not *repentance*. That word might make you picture a picket line of people holding signs that read "Turn or burn. *Repent or die*." Or maybe you hear the words of a scolding Sunday school teacher when you think of repentance. I was definitely in this category for most of my life. The idea of repentance was terrifying. But in the last few years, the word *repentance* has become one of my favorites. I know, I know, this word carries some weight. It may make us think about shame and fear, condemnation and judgment. And yet, Scripture tells us that the kindness of the Lord is what leads us to repentance (Romans 2:4). So where are we getting it wrong? My belief is that when most of us choose to repent, we're not thinking of our repentance as a means to find freedom.

When I was a kid, I asked Jesus into my heart and repented of my sins so that I could be born again. I was four and, honestly, I just didn't want to go to hell. I was not about the fiery place; I wanted the streets of gold. Salvation was not a hard sell for me. I may not have felt the entire weight of conviction I feel now as an adult, but the truth is that in that moment, the Holy Spirit filled my body, and I became a child of God. Just like that. I remember telling all my friends about the new relationship I had. To this day, sharing the salvation message is one of my greatest callings. I fell in love with the goodness of God, and I thought I would never sin again. The reality, of course, was that I still lived in a flawed and fleshly body. Repentance is never a one-and-done process; it needs to become a lifestyle.

Repentance means turning in a new direction. It means leaving our old way of living to go a new way or walking away from the things that keep us bound so we can pursue a new path. Repentance means acknowledging our sin and its effects and then *choosing* to move away from it because we know our sin is keeping us from deeper intimacy with God. When we repent, we choose closeness to our Father over the temptation of sin— and that closeness offers us a way of hope and life and freedom. If we desire to live fully alive, awakened to all God has for us, repentance is our best friend.

When you acknowledge your need before God, you begin the process of repentance, and the fruit of the Spirit can begin to grow within you. Now, some areas of sin in your life may be easy to turn from, while others will involve a lifetime of struggle. One such struggle, which requires a constant state of repentance, is our unbelief. We see an example of this in Mark 9:24, when a father desperate for his child's healing cried out, "Lord, I believe; help my unbelief!" (paraphrased). We are constantly in need!

My professor Dr. Dan Allender teaches that repentance is an all-the-time thing that continually brings us back into the intimacy God has for us. I remember hearing him in class refer to repentance as an "invitation to the party." When I first heard this from him, my ears immediately perked up. Party? Yes, please! He then shared the story of the prodigal son found in Luke 15:11–32. I'm sure you know the story. I've heard it almost my whole life.

There was a man who had two sons. The younger one said to his father, "Father, give me my share of the estate." So he divided his property between them.

Not long after that, the younger son got together all he had, set off for a distant country and there squandered his wealth in wild living. After he had spent everything, there was a severe famine in that whole country, and he began to be in need. So he went and hired himself out to a citizen of that country, who sent him to his fields to feed pigs. He longed to fill his stomach with the pods that the pigs were eating, but no one gave him anything.

When he came to his senses, he said, "How many of my father's hired servants have food to spare, and here I am starving to death! I will set out and go back to my father and say to him: Father, I have sinned against heaven and against you. I am no longer worthy to be called your son; make me like one of your hired servants." So he got up and went to his father.

But while he was still a long way off, his father saw him and was filled with compassion for him; he ran to his son, threw his arms around him and kissed him.

The son said to him, "Father, I have sinned against heaven and against you. I am no longer worthy to be called your son."

But the father said to his servants, "Quick! Bring the best robe and put it on him. Put a ring on his finger and sandals on his feet. Bring the fattened calf and kill it. Let's have a feast and celebrate. For this son of mine was dead and is alive again; he was lost and is found." So they began to celebrate.

—Luke 15:11–24

This time, when I heard the story from Dr. Allender, it struck me differently as he painted the picture of the son walking back to his father's house after squandering his inheritance. The son's biggest hope is to be accepted back as a servant in his father's home. A *servant*. He had come to the end of himself, eating slop with pigs, so in his mind anything had to be better. As he walks toward his father's house, though, he sees his father *running* toward him with arms wide open, ready to receive him with an embrace. The son begins to explain his situation, but before he can get all the words out, his father calls for a huge feast to be prepared and for the best food to be made. This is not what the son was expecting. This is a full-on, bells-and-whistles, welcome-back party! It's the opposite of the servanthood he'd expected. The son had a whole speech prepared, but the father is just happy to have his son home. The son's return restored the intimacy of his relationship with his father, and his father wants to throw a party to celebrate this restoration.

This is repentance—an invitation to the party. This is the continual posture of the heart of God. Your return, your repentance is his delight. There are so many things I do wrong, so many days I must come before the Lord, regretful speech in hand, but before I can get the words out . . . God is preparing for party time! The prodigal son story shows us the heart of a good father and the heart of a broken but beautiful child. This story is our story. It shows that we need repentance because we need care and rescue.

We have many needs. We need care and kindness—and this is what we receive through repentance. To associate repentance with shame and condemnation is to miss the whole point of the story. I think the Enemy has tried as hard as he can to redefine repentance in our minds, because if we fully embraced the power of repentance, he could never keep us from true freedom again.

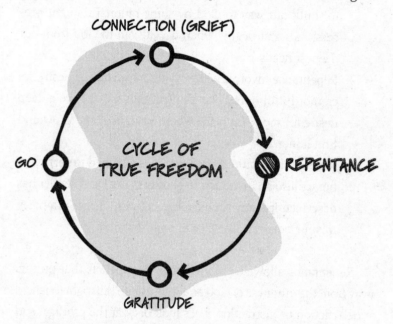

Repentance allows the fullness of our humanity to meet the fullness of God's divinity. We must see our needs as opportunities to repent and thereby gain freedom from whatever has entangled our spirits. So, friend, let's allow the Holy Spirit to help us unlearn the belief that having needs makes us less spiritual or that having to constantly repent means we don't have enough faith. May we not believe these lies! This is what God offers: he welcomes us time and time again to the feast, back into the fold, to behold his glory. Repentance is our invitation to the party.

Keep the following three truths in mind when you think about repentance as exemplified in the story of the prodigal son:

1. Repentance starts deep within us, stemming from our need to be rescued. We cannot meet this need through our human abilities. Repentance does *not* begin by trying to think our way to God by some rational thought process; rather, it begins when we call out to God from our deepest needs.

2. Repentance involves acknowledging we have a desire we cannot fulfill ourselves. Our gut tells us, "I have a deep desire for more—a place where I can heal and grow and find honor."

3. Repentance requires grief, which is attached to sorrow— but it's also an invitation to goodness. As Dr. Allender has described it many times in his lectures, "There is a party in your honor, in the face of your dishonor."

Repentance allows us to challenge false beliefs that pull us away from the kindness of God and lead us into self-righteousness or destruction or distraction. Let's look back at the prodigal son passage, this time taking note of the older brother. We find the older brother out in the field after his younger brother has returned. Curious about the fuss, he asks one of the servants why there is music playing and what's going on. When he learns that his younger brother has returned,

> The older brother became angry and refused to go in. So his father went out and pleaded with him. But he answered his father, "Look! All these years I've been slaving for you and

never disobeyed your orders. Yet you never gave me even a young goat so I could celebrate with my friends. But when this son of yours who has squandered your property with prostitutes comes home, you kill the fattened calf for him!"

"My son," the father said, "you are always with me, and everything I have is yours. But we had to celebrate and be glad, because this brother of yours was dead and is alive again; he was lost and is found."

—Luke 15:28-32

We often think of repentance as being for the really messed-up folks, the ones who have clearly strayed off the path of righteousness. *Those* people, we think, are the ones who need daily repentance. We think to ourselves, "I'm not *that* bad!" I love that Scripture doesn't leave us with just the story of the prodigal son but also introduces us to the older brother, who we might see as the "really good" Christian boy. He's the one who knows all the words to the worship songs, serves every weekend in his community, has books of the Bible memorized . . . you get the picture. The older brother's story speaks directly to those with a religious spirit—a spirit that says, "I'm better than *them*."

This story gives us insight into both the father and the older brother. I was struck by the way the father *pleads* with his older son. The father goes out to have a conversation with his son, pleading with him to come inside and enjoy the goodness of his brother's return. But the son's stubbornness, self-righteousness, and pride keep him from celebrating that his brother is back. We see the heart of the father in this interaction. He is filled with compassion for his older son as he invites him to join the party and reminds him that he has always had access to his father's house.

Religion can mess people up at times, causing them to operate on a basis of good deeds rather than from a place of humble need. My heart breaks more for the older brother than it does for the prodigal son. The prodigal's sin was obvious. It was clear he was a mess and in need. But the older brother's heart isn't revealed for what it really feels until the moment with his father arrives. The older brother is motivated not by a heart of submission to and love for his father but rather by a desire for accolade and position. His need is to "repent of his religion"—to repent of the mindset that he's superior to his brother and deserves praise and reward for his good deeds.

It can be hard to see our need to repent of our religion, because the world, our families, our churches, and our friendships may all be benefiting in some way from the good deeds we're doing. The people and organizations we serve thrive off our ability to work and achieve, and we thrive off the praise we get in return. It can be difficult to discern whether we're operating out of pride or self-righteousness—or perhaps just plain vanity because we love the praise we get for a job well done. The problem, of course, is that we will never be fulfilled if we're operating from one of these motivations. We will find ourselves bound to public opinion, comparing our gifts and achievements with those of others, and questioning our value if we aren't seen as the best.

Both the prodigal son and the older brother need to repent; they both find themselves bound to behaviors or beliefs that offer temporary satisfaction but leave them in bondage. Repentance—if they choose to repent—would allow both of them to return to the father's table with honor, to rejoice with each other, and to function out of a tended-to heart rather than brokenness.

Repentance is the key to surrendering what is keeping you bound so you can walk toward all God has for you.

Now that you have an idea of what repentance is, let's name what it *isn't:* penance. If repentance is an invitation to the party, penance is a cover charge you pay to get in. Wouldn't you much rather be invited to a friend's party at no charge than be told you can come if you pay? A mindset focused on penance says, "I want to be in control. I can pay for my crime and show why I should be 'let back in.'" But penance can never restore your connection with God.

Penance keeps you bound in a cycle of trying to earn your freedom, all the while heaping shame and guilt upon you for never measuring up. It's exhausting and keeps you far from the intimacy you long for with your Savior. If you believe you must somehow pay or make up for the crimes you have committed, you won't recognize your need for God. Far from his grace, you won't understand his love and you'll view Jesus as an overlord demanding a price you can never pay. A mindset of penance overlooks the glorious sacrifice Jesus made on your behalf, and because of this, penance is exactly where the Enemy wants to keep you. If repentance is God's path to redemption, then penance is the Enemy's tool to keep you forever broken.

Unlike penance, repentance creates gratitude in our hearts. And I don't mean forced gratitude, which we're often encouraged to muster up in church culture. Now, don't get me wrong, I love a good gratitude journal. But here I'm talking about the deep gratitude we feel when we repent of our sin and receive forgiveness and connection with God. In that place—where we are seen and known and loved—we experience true gratitude as we begin to grasp the bounty and beauty God offers us. We find ourselves saying from the depth of our soul, "You held me, you saw me, you welcomed me . . . even though I had turned away." We experience God becoming a shield around us. Our eyes open to a world of wonder and delight, allowing desire and hope to rise within us.

> *Dear Lord, speak to me. Help me know the areas(s) where repentance will free me from bondage. Check my pride, my self-righteousness, and even my unnamed brokenness. I want off the penance cycle and into the cycle of true heart transformation through the steps of repentance. I feel the sorrow of my actions, and I also see the hope you offer as you wait for my heart's return. As I pause and listen, bring to my mind an area of my life where I need to start my journey of repentance with you today. In Jesus's name, amen.*

CHAPTER 24

SEEING GOODNESS

Have you ever kept a gratitude journal? These journals were very popular in the culture I grew up in—and they still kinda are. I see many people writing about, singing about, and relying on the power of gratitude. These people believe that if you want to change your story and learn to be more grateful for what you have and what God has done, you must continually remind yourself of things for which you are grateful. I agree with this . . . partly. While it's great to be grateful, true healing isn't as easy as writing down that you're happy to have a car, your kids, a job, or even God's love. This practice may be a wonderful idea, but I don't think it can lead to healing on its own.

No matter how hard we try, our attempts at gratitude often wane during the hardships of life. We may feel beat down, disheartened, overwhelmed, angry, cheated, overlooked . . . the list goes on. If we rely solely on "thinking good thoughts," we limit our ability to heal. Have you ever been sharing with someone about a difficult season, and the person responded with something like "Yeah, that's hard, but look at all you have to be grateful for!" Didn't you want to punch them in the face when they said that? No, just me? I mean, yeah, me neither . . .

Being reminded that we should be grateful for what we have is not bad, but it can also belittle the pain we may be experiencing. We can be grateful and still be hurting. The "think good thoughts" mantra can leave us feeling guilty, unseen, and confused and frustrated as to why we can't "get over it." Gratitude is not a Band-Aid to fix our problems; it is the outcome that occurs when we are honest about the pain in our stories but have received the loving kindness we need. Gratitude emerges from the ashes of brokenness when our brokenness is met with care.

We Christians love Easter! It's like the Super Bowl of the church year. Don't get me wrong. I love Easter too, but I think we as followers of Jesus can sometimes believe the false idea that life with Jesus will be all resurrection all the time. This is not true. A relationship with Jesus involves salvation through his death, burial, and then resurrection. We often forget that death precedes the resurrection. Pain came before redemption and salvation. And it doesn't end with the resurrection either. Once we receive new life in Christ, we then begin becoming more like Christ. This means dying to the snares that are keeping us bound, surrendering our lives before the King, and allowing him access to the places in our lives that need healing so we can grow in our sanctification. Even Jesus had to die, wait, and *then* rise! It's in our dying that we experience his comfort. It's in our waiting that we encounter his faithfulness. It's in our stories of harm that we will eventually see his goodness as he redeems those stories.

When we have gone through the process of connecting with ourselves, with God, and with others, and have repented of the

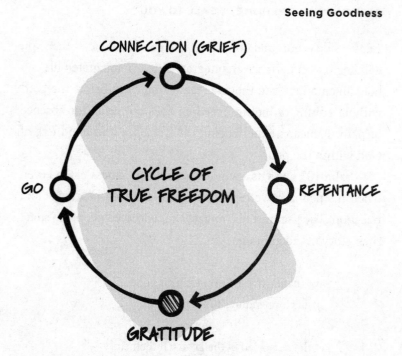

CONNECTION (GRIEF)

GO

CYCLE OF
TRUE FREEDOM

REPENTANCE

GRATITUDE

aspects of our lives that have kept us distant from God, only then can we begin to fully understand the goodness of God. It's as if a supernatural gratitude comes over us and we see our story through different eyes. Sure, we still see the harm and the pain, but now we can also see the goodness of God. We can see his presence when we thought we were alone. We can see him defending us when we felt rejected. We can see him nurturing us when wounds caused by our mothers ran deep. We can see him beside us when we felt the absence of our earthly fathers.

As you become who you were created to be and experience the redemption of your story, the result is a life that can hold both hurt and hope—and experience both grief and goodness. You will be able to name your fears without shame, and alongside your fears will be an increasing sense of faith that God has you. When you find yourself able to hold the complexities of life side by side—hurt *and* hope, grief *and* goodness, etc.—then you will begin to experience an integrated life. An integrated life can hold all emotions and thoughts and bring them before the Lord without editing or hiding. Freedom does not mean the absence of pain; it means experiencing the presence and goodness of God within the pain.

Psalm 107 gives us a window into the goodness of God even when his people have rebelled and experienced heartache and rejection. The psalmist encourages the redeemed people to share their story of redemption:

> Give thanks to the LORD, for he is good;
>> his love endures forever.

> Let the redeemed of the LORD tell their story—
>> those he redeemed from the hand of the foe,
> those he gathered from the lands,
>> from east and west, from north and south.
>
> **—Psalm 107:1-3**

The psalmist wants us to remember our stories and share them. We will get into that more a bit later, but I think it's important here to notice God's response in the midst of the people's pain and sin. When the people cried out, God saved and delivered them. The psalm goes on to describe how God has walked people out of a variety of troubles. These Scriptures show some of the most painful experiences of humanity and God's response. Even when he is angry due to the actions of his people, his goodness and mercy prevail.

The goodness of God within our stories enables us to

experience true gratitude. We see and feel and know this goodness when we offer our whole selves to him. He cannot separate
himself from his goodness; it is the essence of who he is. And
that goodness is within you. That goodness is for you. That
goodness will propel you to hope again, to dream again, to play
again. Psalm 27:13–14 is often recited in my heart and home. It
is a confident saying, one that reassures me of God's promises
and care for my heart and story:

> I remain confident of this:
>> I will see the goodness of the LORD
>> in the land of the living.
> Wait for the LORD;
>> be strong and take heart
>> and wait for the LORD.

In this psalm, David expresses confidence that he will see
the Lord's goodness within his lifetime. This comes on the
heels of his describing examples of harm and heartache he has
endured in life. But he won't lose heart, he will hold to the truth,
and he won't keep God out of the hard places of his life—rather,
he will seek God in all of it. It's with this posture that he can see
the goodness of God even in the midst of the brokenness. David
encourages us not to just wait on God, but to stay strong and
take courage as we wait.

It takes courage to become who God created you to be. It
takes courage to face the stories that have kept you bound. It takes
courage to grieve and repent. But numerous Scriptures assure us
that God will meet us and offer comfort and rescue. It's from this
place of confidence that we can see the goodness of God within

our story. When this begins to happen, you are on your way to experiencing the life you have read about—the fully alive life. This life is one of abundance, not because you have all the things or have avoided all the pain, but because you see and experience God's goodness no matter the circumstance.

Now that leads to true gratitude!

> *Dear Lord, my gratitude comes not because I've tried to manufacture it but because I have brought my whole self to you and you have shown loving-kindness toward me. My gratitude comes from an overflow of my heart. When I lack gratitude, help me to name where my heart is in need so you can become the wellspring of comfort that will move me to gratitude. In Jesus's name, amen.*

CHAPTER 25

YOUR HEART'S DESIRE

On your journey to healing, there are certain steps you may need to revisit time and time again. When life hits hard, connection, repentance, and gratitude will be essential. And although you won't experience full freedom this side of heaven, you can still become more like Christ and live the life God is calling you to. One way you can do this is by embracing the particularities of your story. And you don't do this work just to keep all your healing and freedom to yourself. When you begin to heal, something will rise within you. Dr. Allender often speaks of this "something" in his lectures; he refers to it as your "Hell no, not on my watch will I continue to let this happen on the land." This "hell no" is born from the places of your story where you were once wounded and stuck but have now experienced freedom. You don't want anyone else to experience what you have experienced. You have tasted hope within your own story and now you want to offer that same hope to the world around you. This is where godly desire begins—a desire that drives creativity and play.

Godly desire is the antithesis of what I'll call demand.

Demand is an internal sense that if we don't perform or achieve or play the role we're expected to play, we will lose belonging. Demand says, "I will lose love and worth if I don't do what's expected." Those of us who haven't been honest about our pain often function out of demand. This means that our actions are driven by a sense of demand and burden rather than coming from a joy-filled desire to live into God's purposes for our lives. Demand leaves us constantly trying to keep up and stay worthy.

The beauty of coming back to who you were created to be through honest connection with yourself, God, and others is that your sense of demand decreases, and godly desire rises within you. You start wanting to create simply because you *want* to. You become so filled with the love of Jesus and aware of his heart for you that you begin to have that same heart for other people. Godly desire awakens you to life in full color; it takes the gifts you've had since you were young and focuses those gifts on your calling.

The word *desire* often gets a bad rap; the idea of desire may be equated only to lust and sin. Even as a young girl, I remember hearing that if I gave in to desire, I would be swept away by sin. Maybe that was just my experience, but I've met many others who are afraid to feel any kind of desire because of what it might awaken in them. Of course, there are certain desires of the flesh that we want to avoid, but if we only speak of desire in a negative context, we ignore the existence of God-given desire that can lead us to create beauty and love deeply. This kind of desire drives us to hope and imagine what could be.

Our ability to feel desires is *from* God. He states clearly in Scripture that he desires you! He created man and woman to commune with him, and although sin entered the garden because of human disobedience, God still pursues us (Psalm 139:7–8). His desire is that none should perish, and he holds off his return for this very reason (2 Peter 3:9). It is because of his desire for you that God sent his son (John 3:16). We encounter his desire for goodness and beauty when we see the colors of a sunset or a colorful flower. He created our bodies to enjoy pleasure from everything from intimacy with a spouse to good food. Some religious voices tell us to shut off pleasure and desire; we are told they are from the Enemy. This is the furthest thing from the truth. A life without desire would be a gray, cold, and empty existence, but out of his love for us, God offers us a life full of godly desire and pleasure.

God began all of eternity creating out of pleasure. He created a world filled with beauty, not only within the natural world but also in humanity. This beauty is seen in the curiosity of a child when they make a castle on the seashore. It's found in the moment when someone has an idea that will help make the world a better place. Godly desire flows from a contented heart; it leads us to partner with God to bring goodness into the world.

Scripture contains many examples of God providing the desires of people's hearts. In the Old Testament we see Hannah receiving a child after being barren (1 Samuel 1:1–20) and Hezekiah being healed (2 Kings 20:1–7); in the New Testament we even see Peter miraculously released from prison (Acts 12:1–11). So what does this mean in our lives? Maybe you've spent years praying for something—to have a baby, get a promotion, or see a loved one healed from an illness. Or maybe you've wanted to experience a healthy marriage or financial freedom. Perhaps you've desired these things for years, but they either haven't happened yet or took a really long time. If godly desires are the outcome of a life that is being redeemed, does this mean God will give you everything you want? No, the godly desires that come from a redeemed life focus on fulfilling God's purposes and partnering with him to create a better world. David wrote about God granting our hearts' desires. In Psalm 37 we see that when we surrender our hearts to God and learn to trust him, we begin to want what he wants for our lives:

> Do not fret because of those who are evil
>> or be envious of those who do wrong;
> for like the grass they will soon wither,
>> like green plants they will soon die away.
>
> Trust in the LORD and do good;
>> dwell in the land and enjoy safe pasture.
> Take delight in the LORD,
>> and he will give you the desires of your heart.
>
> **—Psalm 37:1-4**

Many people take this passage out of context and think it means we will get whatever we want. But you and I both know this is not the case—God is not a genie. In this passage, David is encouraging his fellow Israelites to trust and follow God and to commit their lives in obedience to him. Many will oppose them and work to silence them, but God promises his protection as well as the honor that results from a life that delights in the Lord. The desire David refers to is not a desire driven by self-centered personal wants; it's the desire of someone who has been healed by God and therefore has desires that are aligned with God's desires.

Before you were born, God had a purpose in mind for you. He gifted you with a particular set of gifts to be used to usher in his glory on earth. During your childhood, you may have used these gifts without even thinking about it, whether in big ways or small. It came effortlessly and stunningly. You created in ways that made your heart come alive, and those around you experienced delight when you used your gifts. But the Enemy saw this glory and wanted to extinguish its flame. He used various tactics to silence you and make you feel mocked and rejected. He did whatever he could to make you believe that what you bring to the world is stupid, not enough, too much, or unimportant. He was relentless, and for a time you bought his lies. *Then Jesus.* Jesus interrupted the story with his love for you, and he met you in the places where the Enemy had done some of his most insidious work. You experienced grace and love and healing. This is when hope began to rise within you, and a desire to make the world a beautiful place began to emerge. Now, instead of using your gifts without any intentionality, you are invited to partner with the God of the universe to silence the lies of the Enemy in the particular areas where he once tried to silence you. You are invited to join God's mission to offer justice and mercy and love to a world that is lost—just as you once were.

Godly desire drives you even when things seem impossible. Godly desire keeps you up at night, filled with imagination and ideas and dreams. Godly desire makes a way when all seems lost, it gives you courage to face another day, and it allows you to continue to see good even when the world feels as if it's crumbling around you. Godly desire keeps you close to the Father, feeling a sense of intimacy and care and play and imagination.

Peter was arguably one of Jesus's closest disciples. In fact, he was the one about whom Jesus said, "On this rock I will build my church" (Matthew 16:18). Peter was Jesus's ride-or-die, his number two. Before Jesus was betrayed and went to the cross,

Peter told him, "I will be with you till the end. I will never deny you" (paraphrased). This is ironic, because Peter did in fact deny Jesus (Luke 22:54–62). Peter, who was so full of passion and desire to serve and follow Jesus, turned away under pressure. What happened to his passion and desire to stand by his best friend till the end? Fear and then shame squashed it, eventually leading him to return to his old way of life as a fisherman.

But the beauty of this story is that it didn't end there. Jesus interrupted the narrative of Peter's shame. In his resurrected body, Jesus met Peter right where he had first found him. Jesus stood on the shore and called out to Simon Peter and his friends, who were out on a fishing boat. He welcomed them back to shore with a hot breakfast, then offered Peter one of the clearest examples of redemption in Scripture:

> So when they had eaten breakfast, Jesus said to Simon Peter, "Simon, son of Jonah, do you love Me more than these?"
>
> He said to Him, "Yes, Lord; You know that I love You."
>
> He said to him, "Feed My lambs."
>
> He said to him again a second time, "Simon, son of Jonah, do you love Me?"
>
> He said to Him, "Yes, Lord; You know that I love You."
>
> He said to him, "Tend My sheep."
>
> He said to him the third time, "Simon, son of Jonah, do you love Me?" Peter was grieved because He said to him the third time, "Do you love Me?"
>
> And he said to Him, "Lord, You know all things; You know that I love You."
>
> Jesus said to him, "Feed My sheep."
>
> **—John 21:15–17 NKJV**

As Jesus spoke with Peter, he didn't address Peter's act of denial but rather spoke to Peter's heart. Because Peter had denied him three times, Jesus asked him to proclaim his love for him three times. In Peter's story, we can see every level of connection involved in the process of restoration:

Connection to self: Peter understood the reality of his sin and denial.

Connection with God: Peter repented and received comfort and healing.

Connection with others: Peter experienced the human Jesus holding space for his weakness and still loving and desiring relationship with him. Jesus also encouraged Peter to connect with others by loving and serving them.

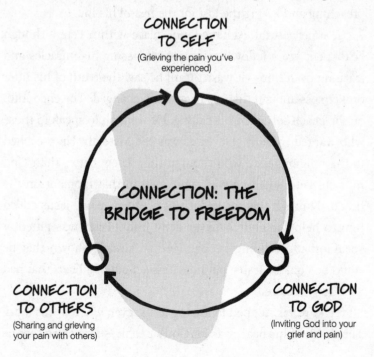

CONNECTION
TO SELF
(Grieving the pain you've
experienced)

CONNECTION: THE
BRIDGE TO FREEDOM

CONNECTION
TO OTHERS
(Sharing and grieving
your pain with others)

CONNECTION
TO GOD
(Inviting God into your
grief and pain)

What a beautiful and powerful story of repentance and restoration!

So what does this story have to do with godly desire? Before Peter's denial of Jesus, his passion was vibrant and on fire—but it faded quickly once the Enemy attacked. He was all too quick to go back to his regular life, feeling forever destined to live in shame, haunted by thoughts of what could have been. But Jesus changed everything. In the moment on the beach, Jesus restored Peter back to who he created him to be. Something shifted in Peter in that moment. His heart's desire aligned with the desires of Jesus when he heard Jesus calling him to bring goodness to the world by feeding and tending Jesus's sheep. How do we know Peter wasn't just having another "passion-filled" moment? Because from this moment on, Peter never stopped serving and preaching and loving the lost for the rest of his life.

A supernatural exchange took place within Peter. Though he'd spent years following Jesus—witnessing his miracles and learning from him—it wasn't until he saw the truth of his utter brokenness and sin that his heart truly changed. The encounter on the beach solidified his calling. He went on to speak to those who wanted to deny that Jesus was the Messiah. He preached to the religious elite who thought they knew better than God himself. Peter's calling was confirmed in that moment on the beach. Through the particularities of Peter's pain, Jesus called him to help the church never deny Jesus. Peter was gifted at speaking and rallying people. He had already shown that he could be bold for Jesus, but now he lived out of a heart that had been fully restored.

Peter never stopped following Jesus, even when it was hard. The desire of his heart was for God's people, so much so that he would deny himself and eventually even die for this desire. This godly desire also drove him to create and dream and imagine a better world.

To think of desire only in a negative sense—related to the sinful desires of the flesh—is to ignore the role godly desire plays in partnering with God to create a better world. Think about all the dreams you once had or perhaps still have. Think of all the ways you have wanted to make the world better. When the lights are out and no one is around, what makes your soul light up?

You may not be able to answer that question yet if the Enemy has given you a lot of doubts. Perhaps he's been telling you how disqualified you are, and the reason you picked up this book was to help you find your true self and your true God-given desires again. If you aren't sure what lights you up, that's okay, but don't settle for a life in gray. Don't dismiss the little one you once were, who offered glimpses of who you were created to be. Show up for your life, and let the riskiness of hope drive you to want more.

Dear Lord, awaken within me the desires of your heart. Help me to dream again and partner with you to create beauty within your world. My desire is to serve you and show the world the hope that lies in you. I believe that you have called and restored me, and it is with this truth in mind that I will serve you. Quench the lies of the Enemy, who wants to keep me silenced; let me be led by your voice alone. In Jesus's name, amen.

CHAPTER 26

THE END (AND THE BEGINNING)

I am so thankful for the chance to reclaim the story of the little girl dancing on the stage. She has helped me remember who I am. She is bold and a little rebellious and free and glory filled. I love her. The reality, though, is I am no longer that innocent. The world has left its mark on me, and I can't help but view life differently now. I am not a child anymore, and as much as I want to warn her and rescue her, the truth is that she has been rescuing me. Underneath all the pain I felt, that little girl still dared to dream, and when my world felt dark, there were moments when she endured and imagined a better life.

How do I integrate all that I've learned on my journey to return to the freedom of that little girl? How do I end a book that feels like a beginning rather than an end? I don't know all the answers, because I don't think our relationships with ourselves or God or each other are supposed to be formulaic. They're complex and dynamic and beautiful and mysterious. At best, we get to share the messiness of the unknown together. We get to let our humanity meet the deity of God right here on earth. Together, we get to explore and play and dream, even when we feel overwhelmed and small. I think there's something to be said for a life that isn't looking for all the answers but instead recognizes that we will never know it all but are held by the God who does.

I was recently speaking at an event in Tennessee, and as I stood on the stage that evening, I felt freedom wash over me. I have had this feeling many times, but this time sticks out in my mind because I paused and felt the Father say, "*This* is what I made you to do." It felt as if *he* was bringing that little girl back onto the stage, but this time I was aware of the sacrifice he had made for me to experience such redemption. For that hour (yes, I speak for a long time!), it was me and Jesus bringing life to the room. I was walking in my calling to make freedom accessible and understandable to others, using my gifts to let the people in that room know they are seen and loved in the most fragile and hidden places of their hearts. I never knew this was going to be my calling, but after the Lord got a hold of me and I spent years healing, a holy desire came over me. I don't want people to ever feel that they can't be honest with God.

As I spoke that night, I watched the Holy Spirit work. He allowed the truth of the stories in the room to come out of hiding and into the light. He worked in hearts, causing tears to fall on behalf of the heartache felt by so many in the room. He moved as men and women felt seen by the creator of the universe for the first time. I watched as hope began to rise for many people whose lives had felt hopeless. This was *the* moment. I knew why I was here, and I was utterly humbled that the desires of my heart were being fulfilled. To gaze upon the face of another image bearer, to see their goodness, and to know God is chasing after them—there is nothing like that feeling in the whole world, and it's the whole reason I wrote this book.

I truly want you free, but not so you can keep freedom to yourself. Freedom is no fun swept under the rug, and I would venture to say that if you are truly experiencing freedom, you won't be able to stay silent. Free people free people. You don't have to speak on stages or sing songs or write poetry. Those are all good things, but they are not the only things. God will direct you and lead you as you go forward into your calling, and, using your gifts and your redeemed story, he will call you to love his kids in ways only you can. Don't limit what your calling is or what you think it "should" be. Don't let comparison (which is never from God) dictate whether you are worthy. Let your freed heart *play*. Let it dream and imagine. Keep it attuned to the sound of the Father's voice, which is full of kindness and hope.

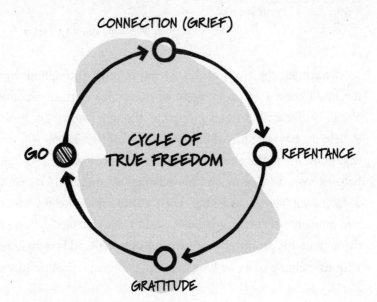

Take joy in the journey, because that is exactly what this is: a journey with no destination but the goal of getting to know the God who loves you and who created you for a purpose. It's a journey to see the truth and expose the lies of an Enemy who is terrified of the glory and abilities God has given you. This journey is full of hardships and holy moments. We can't escape the hard moments, but we can have full assurance that the Lord is with us—that *he* will never leave us or forsake us. When we do have to walk through the valley of the shadow of death, we can have full confidence that he is protecting and guiding us (Psalm 23). Every twist and turn, every heartache and victory—each new step is navigated *with* Jesus. When we feel like we can't take much more, Scripture gives us promises to cling to:

> If your heart is broken, you'll find GOD right there;
> if you're kicked in the gut, he'll help you catch
> your breath.
>
> **—Psalm 34:18 MSG**

I have felt the truth of this Scripture often throughout my life, and I know I will feel it again whenever new hardships come along. Unlike earlier times in my life, though, I now have tools to help me navigate life when my feelings overwhelm me—tools that point me to the care of the Father who created me and that help expose the Enemy and his schemes against me. The pain of facing my story was brutal, but I wanted more for my life. I had moments of tasting goodness, and I knew that God followed through on his promises. Scripture tells us that God is right here with us, helping us as we long for more of him and the abundant life he offers. As you make this journey for yourself, you may have moments when it's hard to catch your breath, or moments when it's hard to see the light as you're traveling through a dark valley, but hold fast. Pursue Jesus; invite him in time and time again. Never settle for less than *all* God created you for.

I have learned that sidestepping our pain keeps us stuck in a cycle that promises hope but leaves us longing. When we allow ourselves to enter into the dark places of our stories, Jesus will reveal his presence and comfort. And experiencing Jesus in the reality of your story is what will ultimately transform your heart.

I think the whole point is to find Jesus *in* the journey—the journey of discovering how good and loving he truly is. The Enemy may have contended for your story, but Jesus contends more. I have faced drug addiction, the suicide of my mother, a broken marriage, a tainted reputation, and more, but God has used all of it for his glory. He took a girl who felt disqualified and who wanted to end it all, and he whispered words of hope in the midst of darkness. All that I endured and all the pain I caused— somehow, in his miraculous way, he redeemed it all. None of what I experienced was in vain. He caused none of it, but he redeemed all of it! When I feel the same old lies of disqualification and inadequacy trying to rear their ugly heads, it's his kindness that keeps me coming back to him. His love gives me courage.

The hope and redemption I've experienced is available for you as well. No matter what your story is, big or small, it matters to God, and it deserves to be tended to and healed. God will walk with you every step of the way, and step by step you will return to who you were created to be! The final book of the Bible shows us a beautiful glimpse of our future:

I heard a voice thunder from the Throne: "Look! Look! God has moved into the neighborhood, making his home with men and women! They're his people, he's their God. He'll wipe every tear from their eyes. Death is gone for good—tears gone, crying gone, pain gone—all the first order of things gone." The Enthroned continued, "Look! I'm making everything new. Write it all down—each word dependable and accurate."

—Revelation 21:3–5 MSG

This is the hope we have. One day our stories will be reclaimed for good. But what do we do with today? Today is not without hope. In Matthew 6:10 (NKJV), Jesus taught his disciples to pray, "Your kingdom come. Your will be done on earth as it is in heaven." Moments of heaven can come to earth—moments when we feel held by the presence of God and know that, although he is enthroned in heaven, he is simultaneously enthroned in our hearts. When Jesus becomes your number one—the one you worship, the one you trust, the one you cry out to, the one you share and grieve with, and the one you sing unto—you heal. And this kind of healing doesn't come and go; this kind of healing transforms you into the person you were always created to be. This is the good news of Jesus.

My prayer is that this book serves as a field guide to help you find your way on the journey. It does not replace the Bible, but it will give you tools to help you more clearly understand the steps you may need to take to experience the abundant life Jesus has for you. By now, you know that suffering is an unavoidable part of life, but my prayer is that you will learn how to engage that suffering with hope and honesty—making friends with godly grief and recognizing the power it can have in healing your story. When that grief is processed well, it will bring about the goodness and gratitude that come from a heart that has been cared for. You will emerge stronger and more alive to who God created you to be.

I will leave you with one of my favorite passages in Scripture. I have held these words close to my heart for many years:

> He has put a new song in my mouth—
> Praise to our God;
> Many will see it and fear,
> And will trust in the LORD.
>
> **—Psalm 40:3 NKJV**

Your mouth will sing a new tune—no longer one of contempt or hopelessness, but a *new* song that will draw others to the goodness of God as they see the redemption he has written into your story. They will put their trust in the Lord because of you!

You are taking the steps to live a life that is free *and* fully alive. This is what you were created for. St. Irenaeus said, "The glory of God is a human being fully alive"—meaning that as you become who God created you to be and fulfill his purposes for your life, you become part of the way God reveals his glory on earth. What an amazing and humbling reality! As you reclaim the story of who you were created to be, never forget that there is no one like you—*not one person.* You are irreplaceable. The world needs your gifts, your silliness, your strength, your tears, your imagination, your boldness, your listening ear . . . the world needs all of you! You, my dear friend, *were meant to be here,* and I can't wait to see how you light up the world with your newfound freedom. I'm here, forever cheering you on, expectantly waiting to see how your journey will help others encounter freedom too.

> *Dear Lord, I am ready. I am ready to walk with you and allow my story of redemption to bring hope to others who cross my path. I have lived far too long forgetting who I was created to be, and I know it is time to emerge with a desire to live out your calling on my life. I will not hide any longer. I will keep offering kindness to my story and allowing you to refine me until the day I get to see you. I lay down my expectation that I am supposed to arrive, but rather I will trust you in the journey. I will honor my story by staying honest with myself and with you, and I will allow a trusted few to walk with me in my calling. I may not know everything you have in store for my future, but it is with great anticipation that I am stepping into a life that is free and fully alive. In Jesus's name, amen.*

NOTES

1. "Suicide Mortality in the United States, 2000–2020," *NCHS: A Blog of the National Center for Health Statistics*, March 3, 2022, https://blogs.cdc.gov/nchs/2022/03/03/6349/.
2. Bessel A. van der Kolk, *The Body Keeps the Score: Brain, Mind, and Body in the Healing of Trauma* (New York: Penguin, 2015), 103.
3. Xiao Nan Lv et al., "Aromatherapy and the Central Nerve System (CNS): Therapeutic Mechanism and Its Associated Genes," *Current Drug Targets* 14, no. 8 (2013): 872–79, https://pubmed.ncbi.nlm.nih.gov/23531112/; Henry Ford Health Staff, "Mood-Boosting Foods: What You Eat Can Affect How You Feel," *EatWell* (blog), Henry Ford Health, March 19, 2018, https://www.henryford.com/blog/2018/03/mood-boosting-foods; Nora D. Volkow, Gene-Jack Wang, and Ruben D. Baler, "Reward, Dopamine and the Control of Food Intake: Implications for Obesity," *Trends in Cognitive Sciences* 15, no. 1 (January 2011): 37–46, https://www.ncbi.nlm.nih.gov/pmc/articles/PMC3124340/.
4. Robert W. Kellemen, *God's Healing for Life's Losses: How to Find Hope When You're Hurting* (Winona Lake, IN: BMH, 2010).
5. J. Douglas Bremner, "Traumatic Stress: Effects on the Brain," *Dialogues in Clinical Neuroscience* 8, no. 4 (2006): 445–61, https://www.ncbi.nlm.nih.gov/pmc/articles/PMC3181836/; Xiao Ma et al., "The Effect of Diaphragmatic Breathing on Attention, Negative Affect and Stress in Healthy Adults," *Frontiers in Psychology* 8 (June 2017): 1–12, https://www.ncbi.nlm.nih.gov

/pmc/articles/PMC5455070/; "Resilience and Child Traumatic Stress," National Child Traumatic Stress Network, accessed January 24, 2023, https://www.nctsn.org/sites/default/files /resources/resilience_and_child_traumatic_stress.pdf; "Stress and the Developing Brain," Center for Early Childhood Mental Health Consultation, accessed January 24, 2023, https://www .ecmhc.org/tutorials/trauma/mod2_3.html; Andrew Huberman, "The Science & Process of Healing from Grief | Huberman Lab Podcast #74," YouTube, May 30, 2022, https://www.youtube.com /watch?v=dzOvi0Aa2EA.

From the Publisher

GREAT BOOKS

ARE EVEN BETTER WHEN THEY'RE SHARED!

Help other readers find this one:

- Post a review at your favorite online bookseller

- Post a picture on a social media account and share why you enjoyed it

- Send a note to a friend who would also love it—or better yet, give them a copy

Thanks for reading!